Denis Savary

jrp|ringier

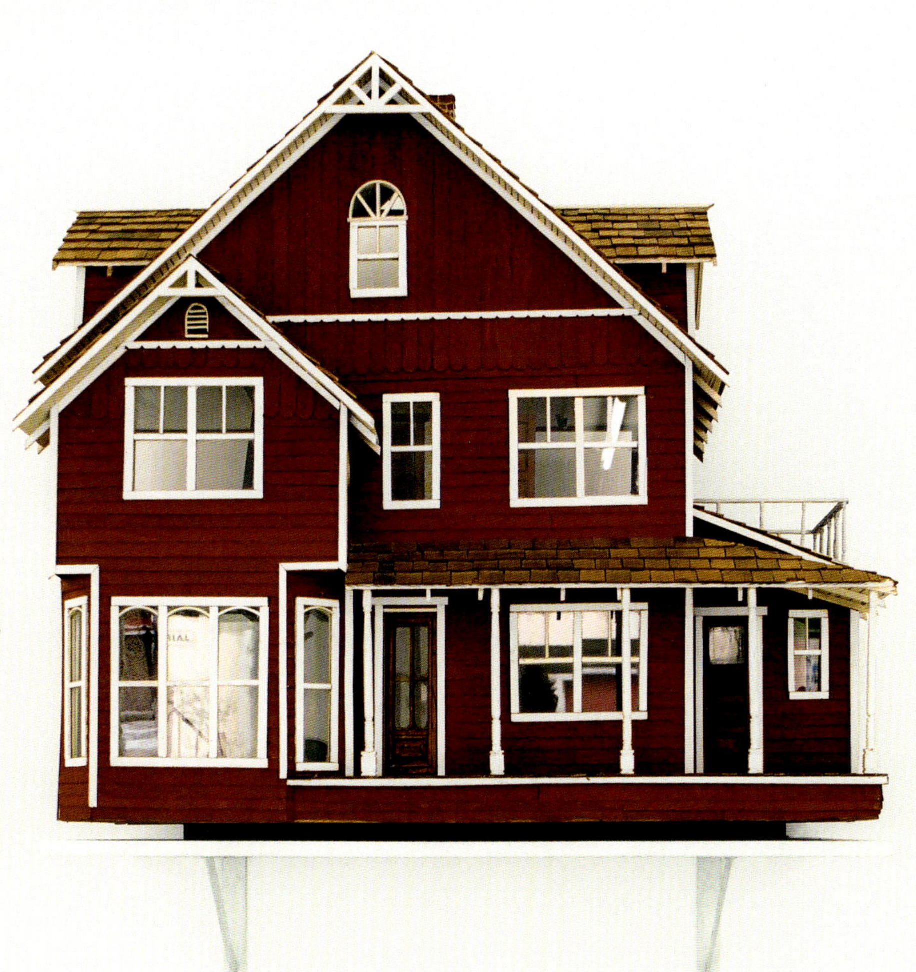

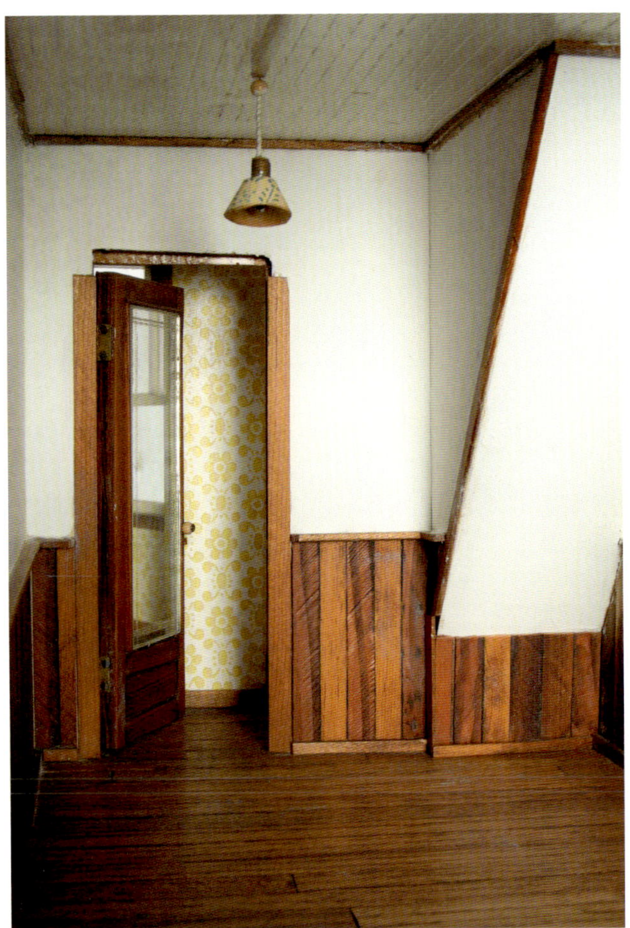

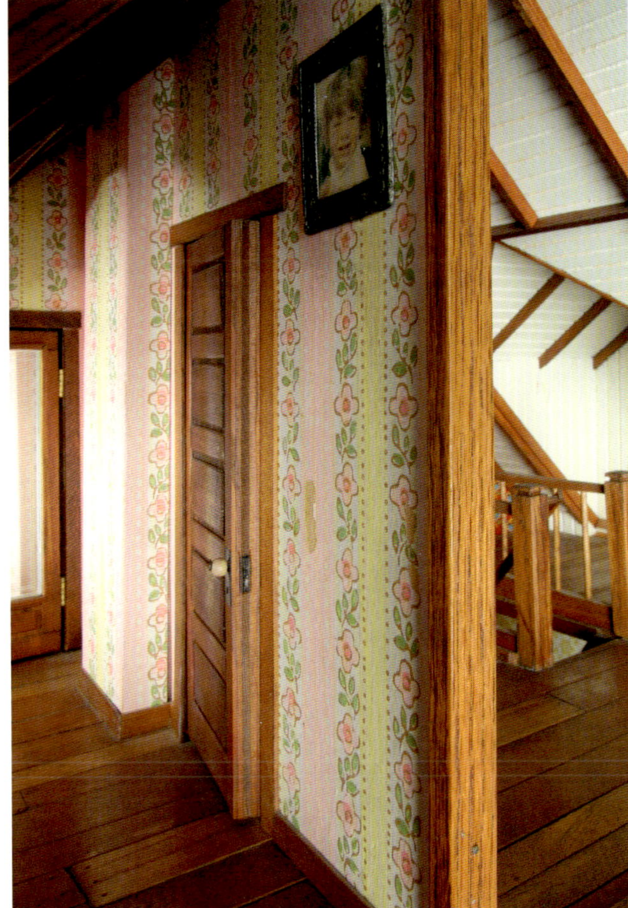

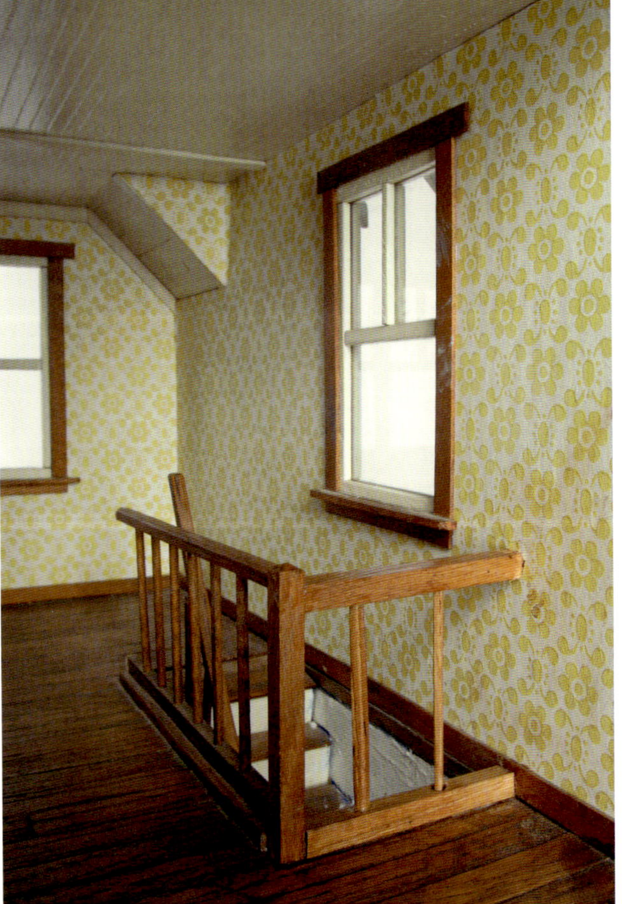

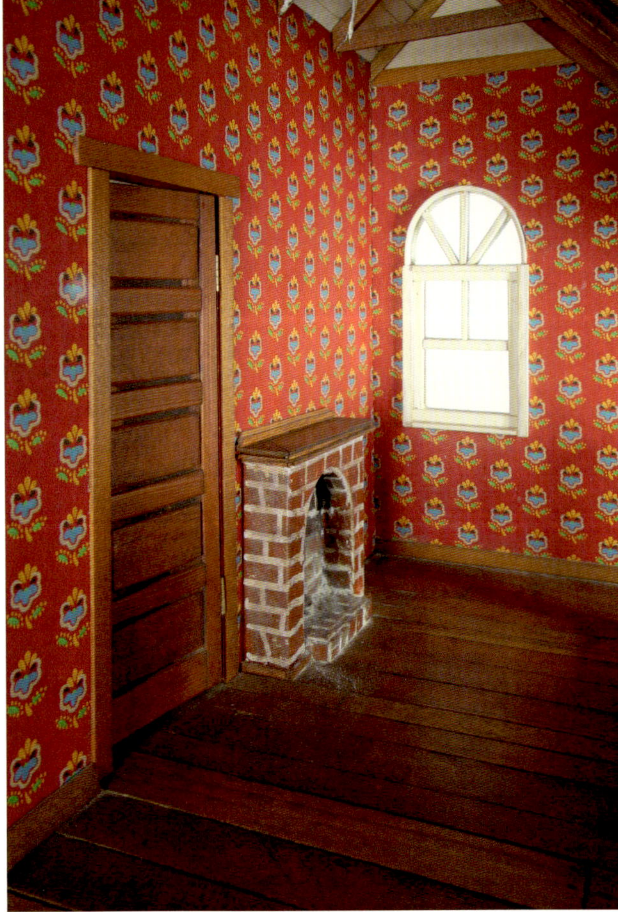

MAISON DE POUPÉE, 2008 (details)

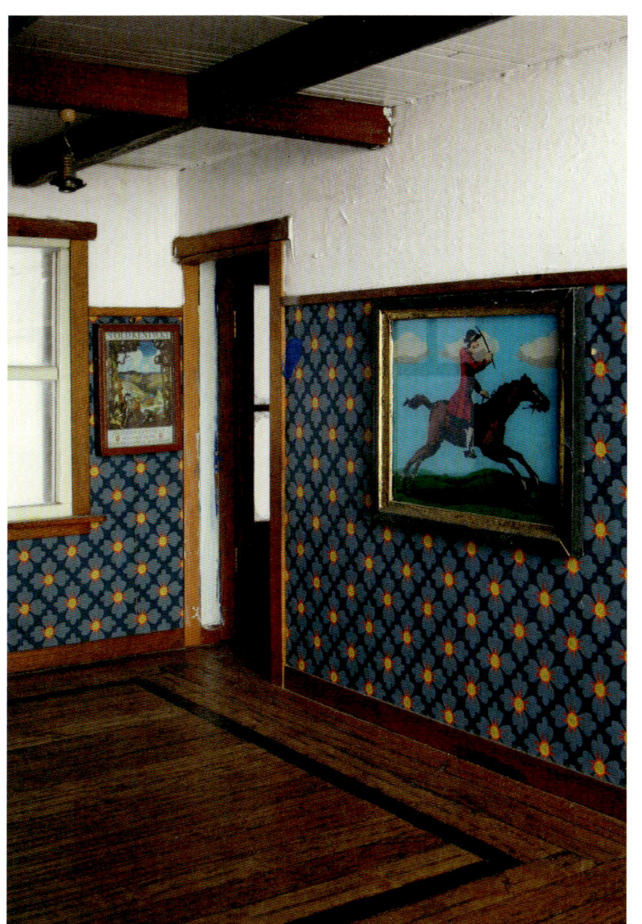
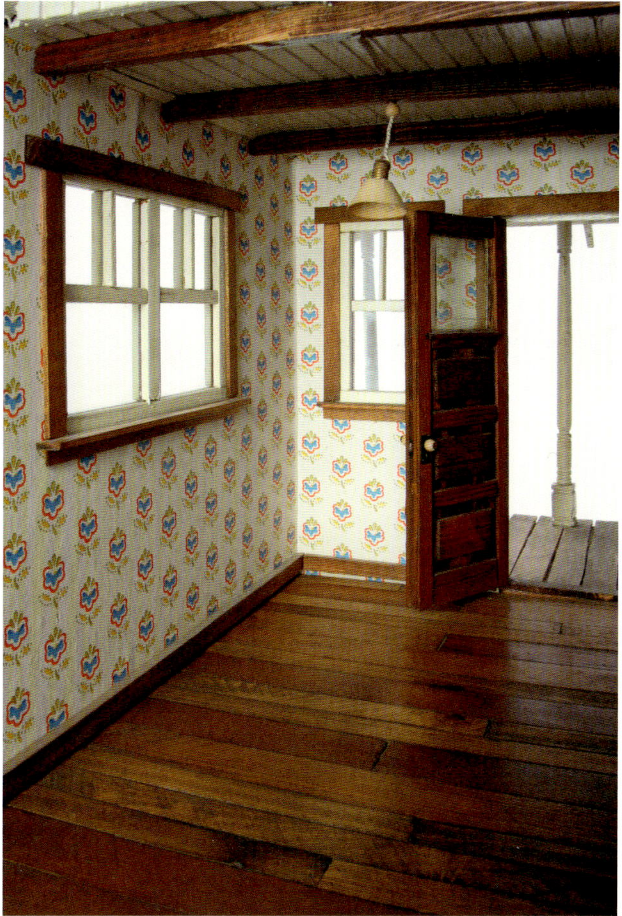
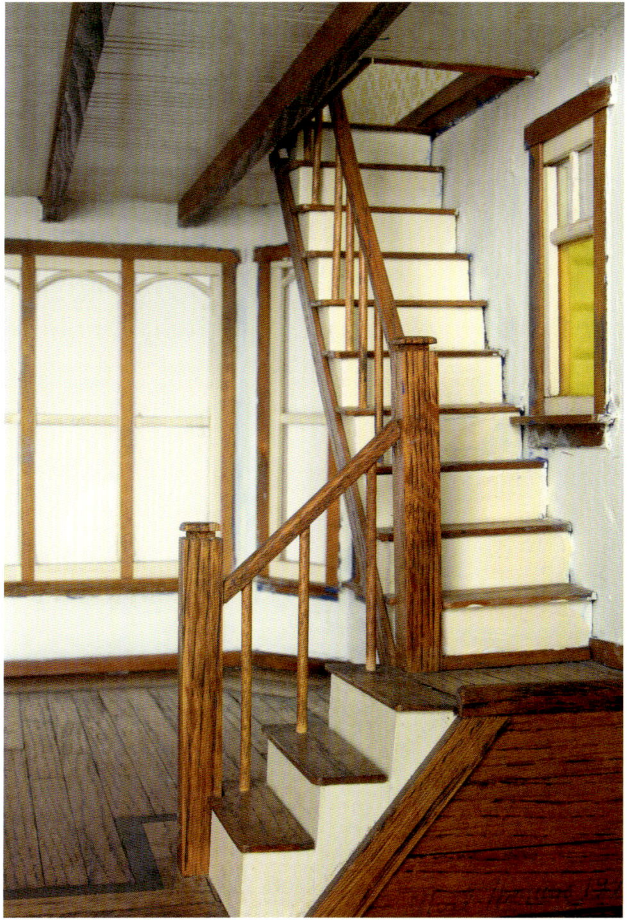
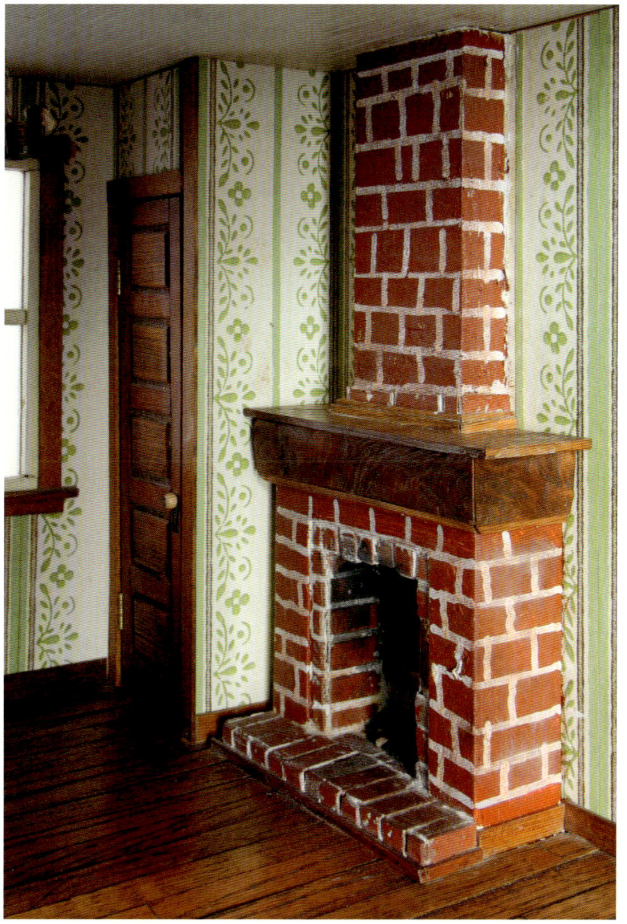

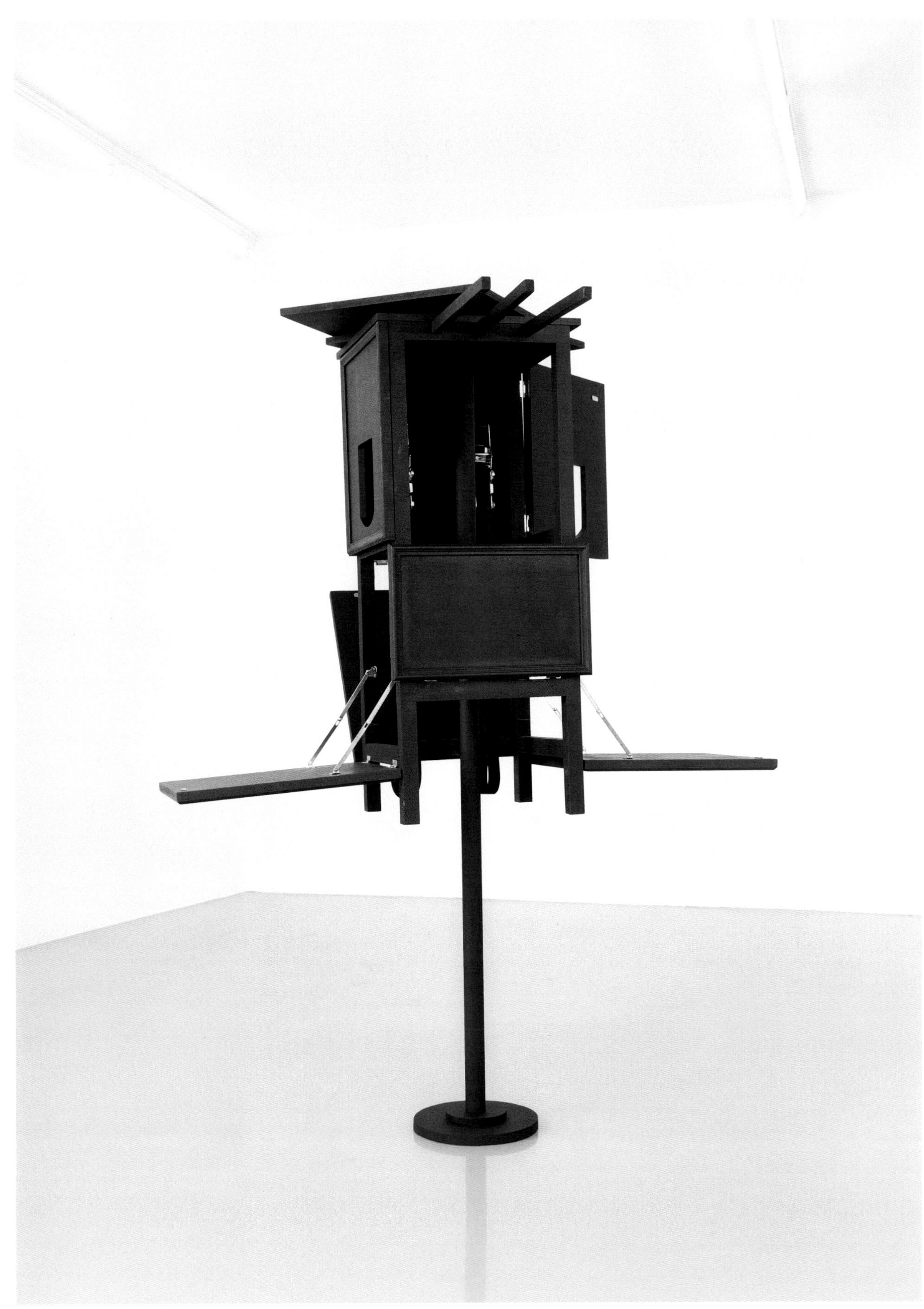

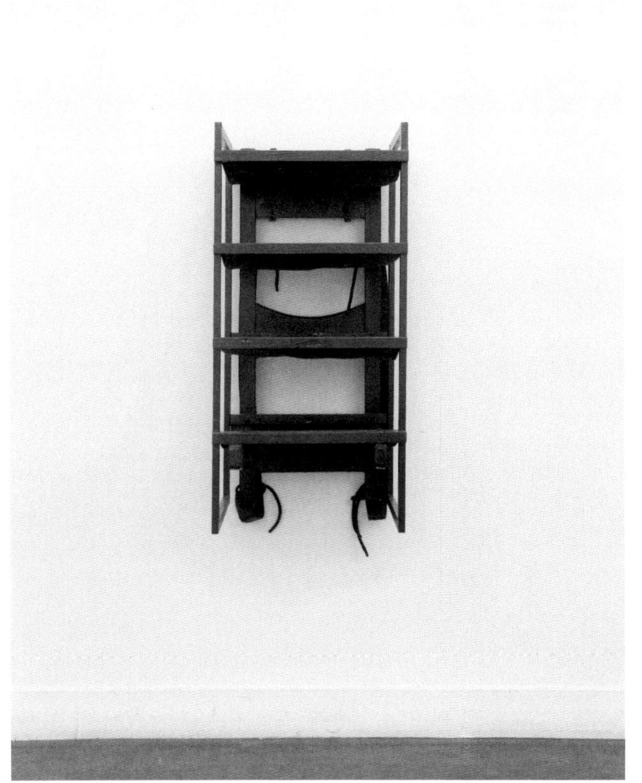

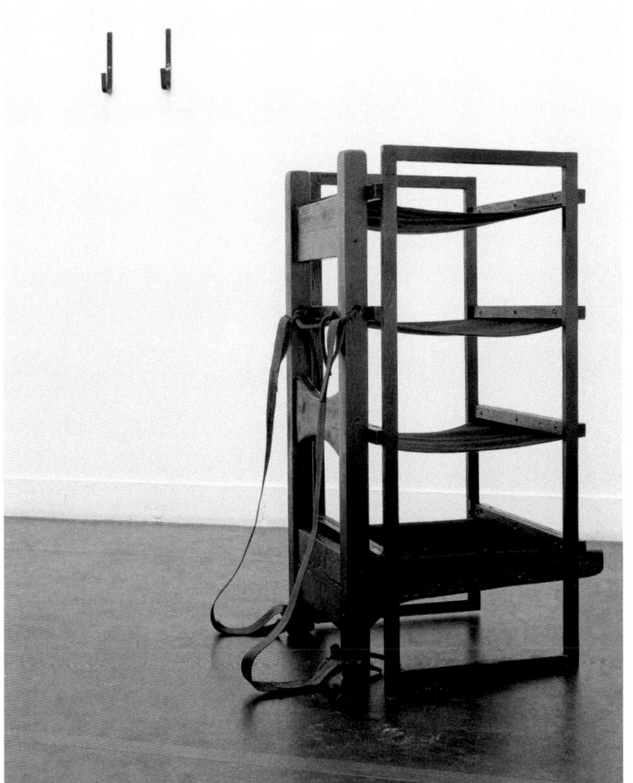

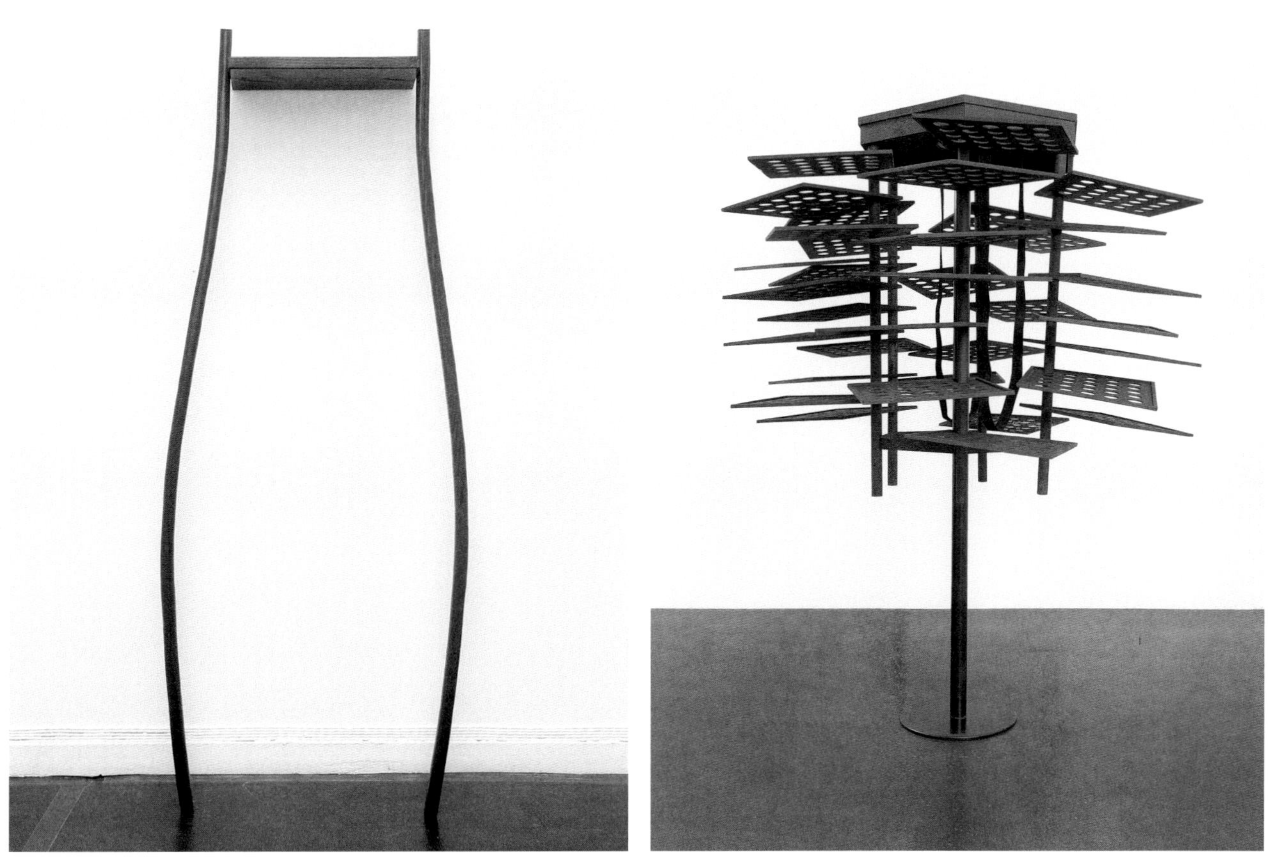

MÉTIER IV (LA GIRAFE), 2010
MÉTIER V (LE PORTEUR D'EAU), 2011

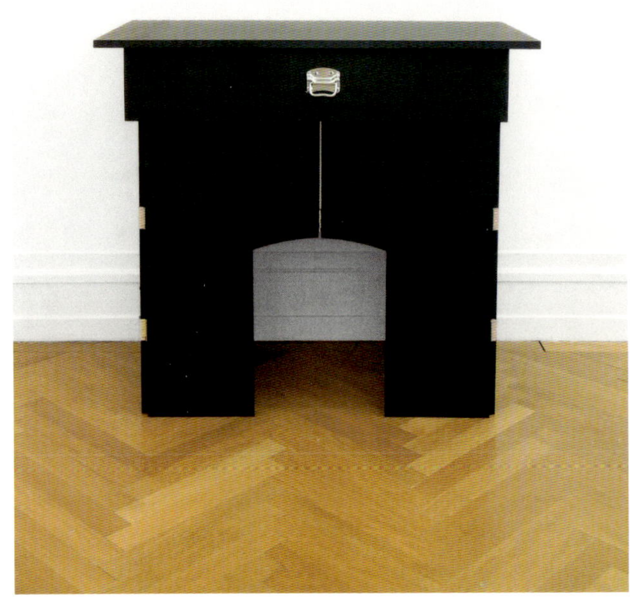

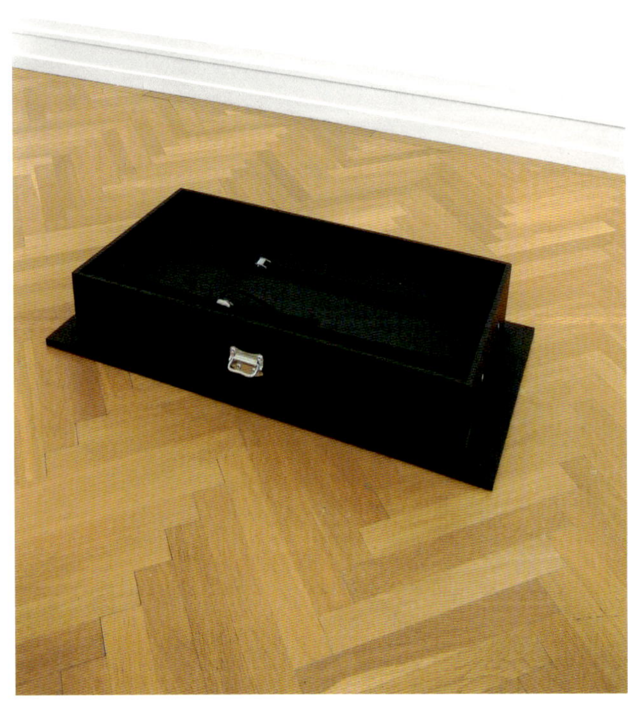

CHEMINÉE, 2011

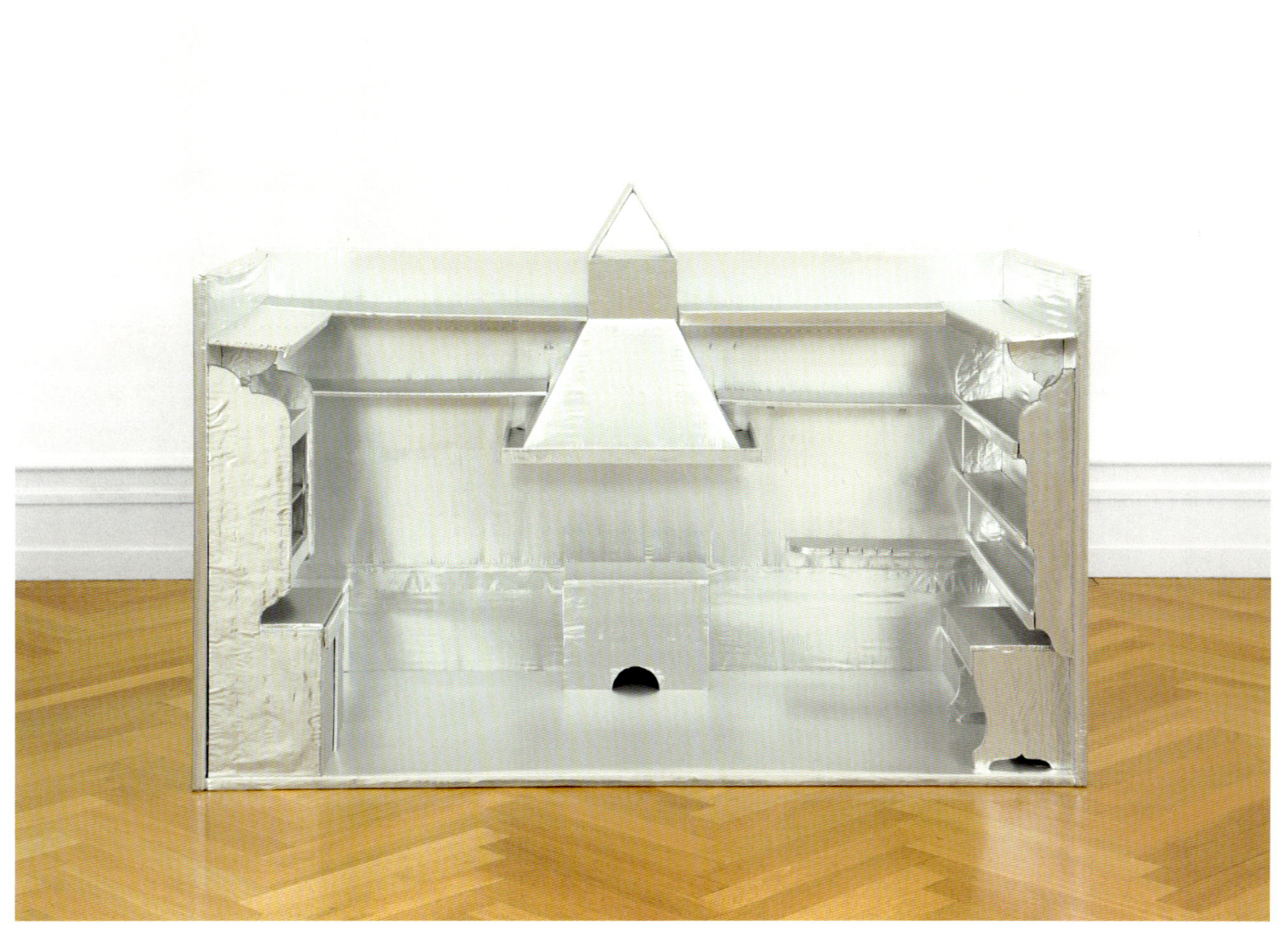

CUISINE, 2012

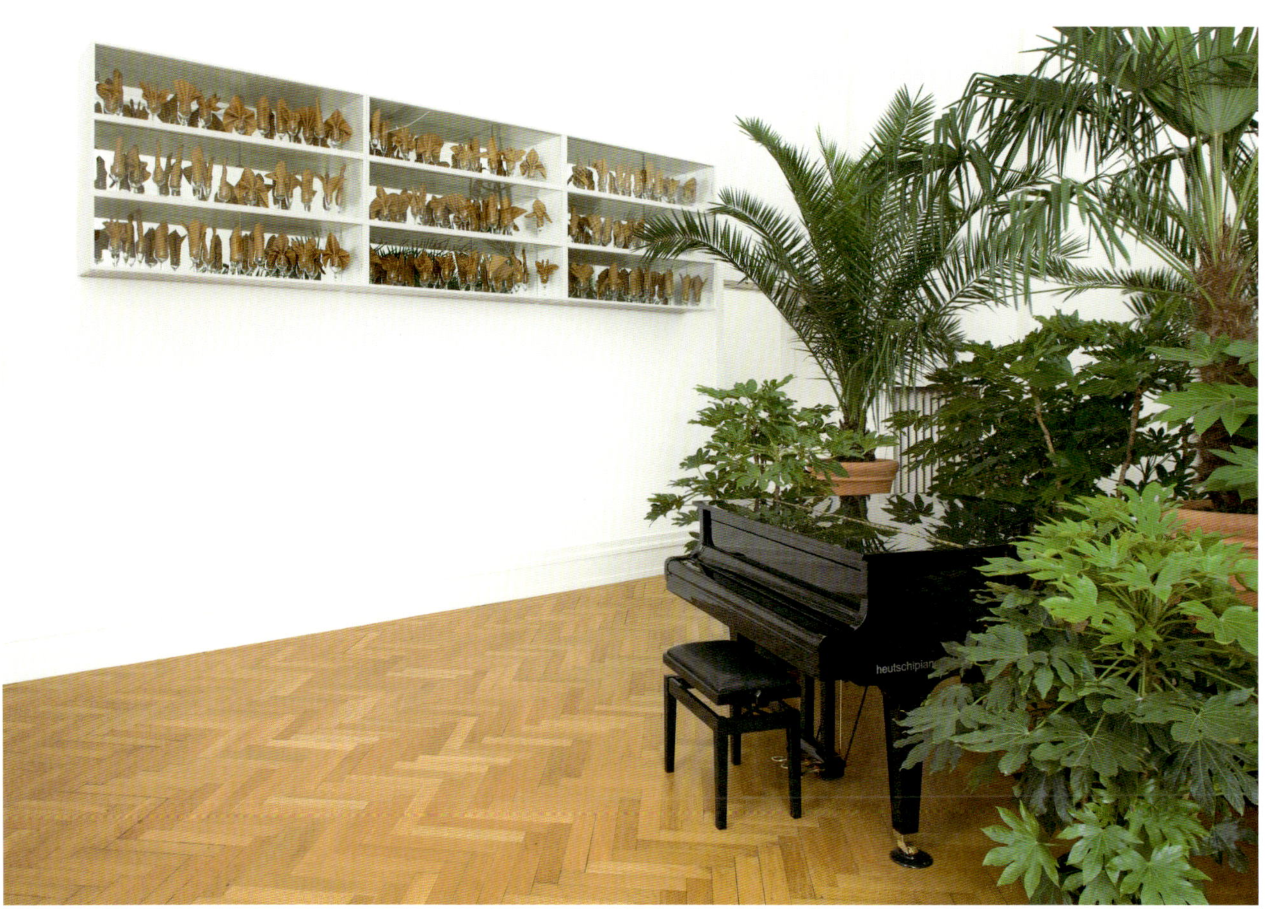

GEORGIA, 2011, exhibition view, *Baltiques*, Kunsthalle Bern, 2012

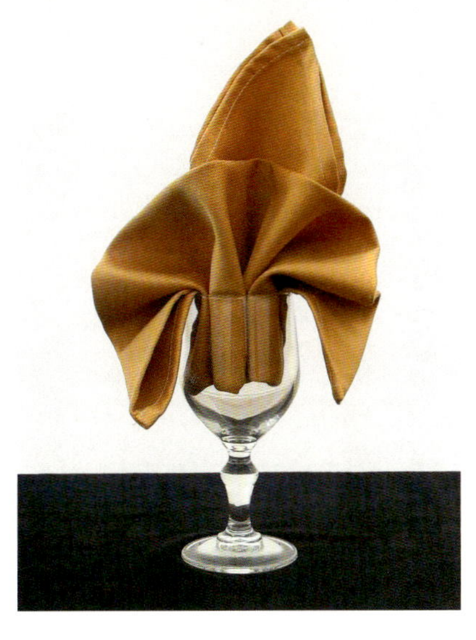
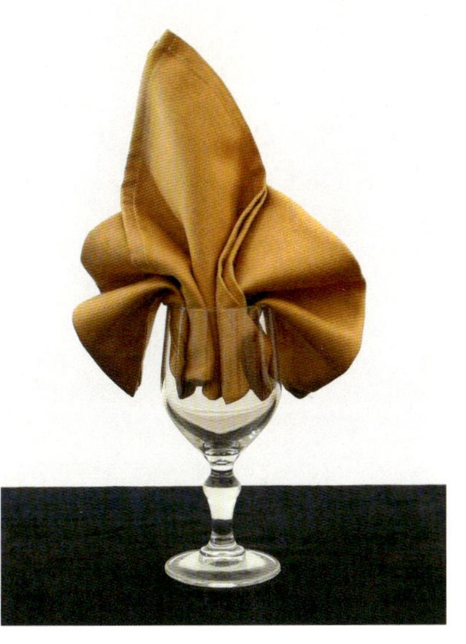
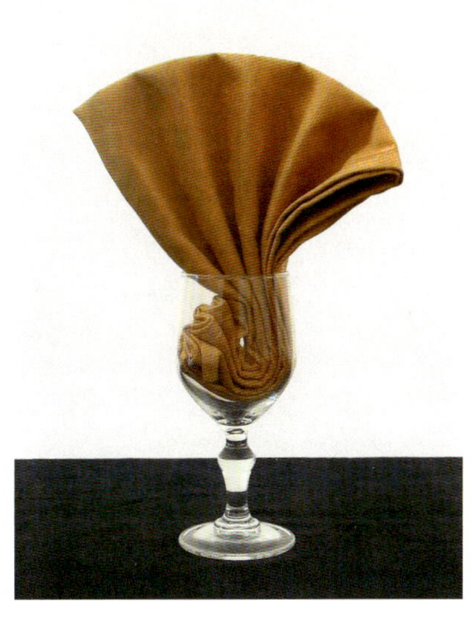
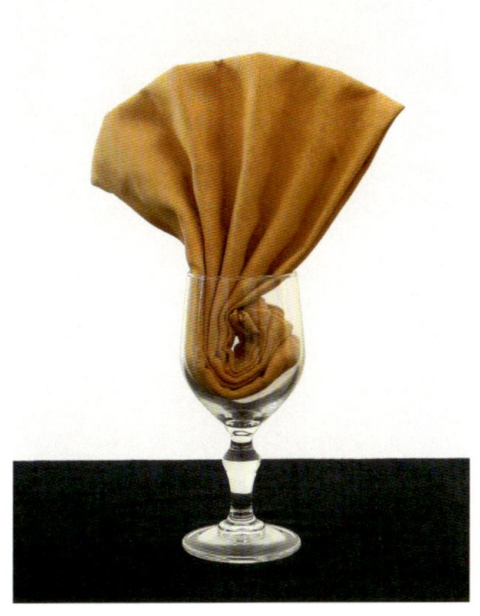
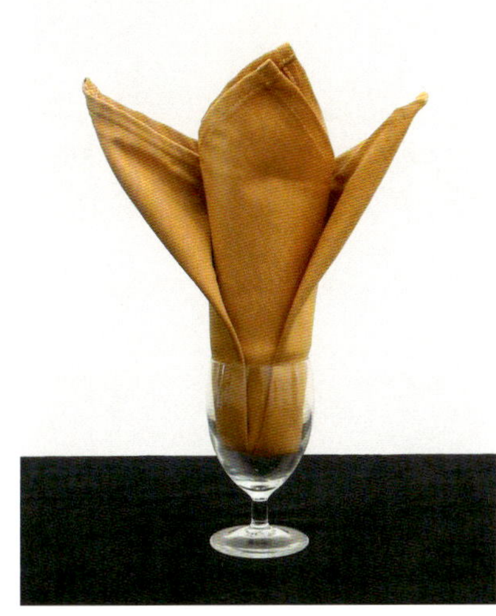
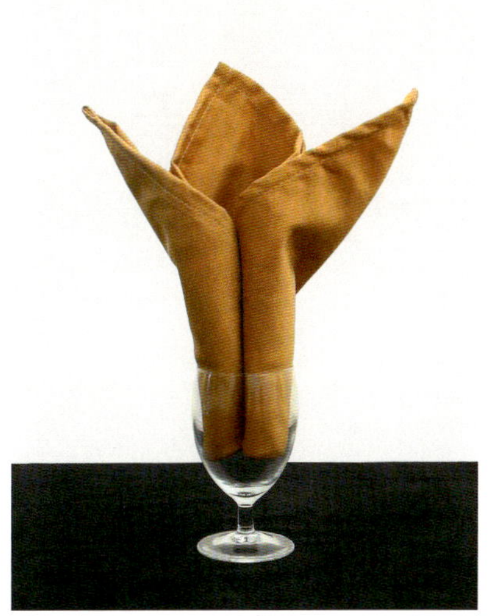
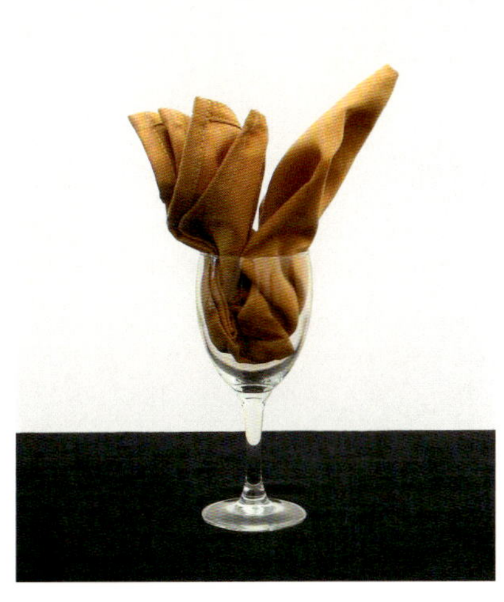
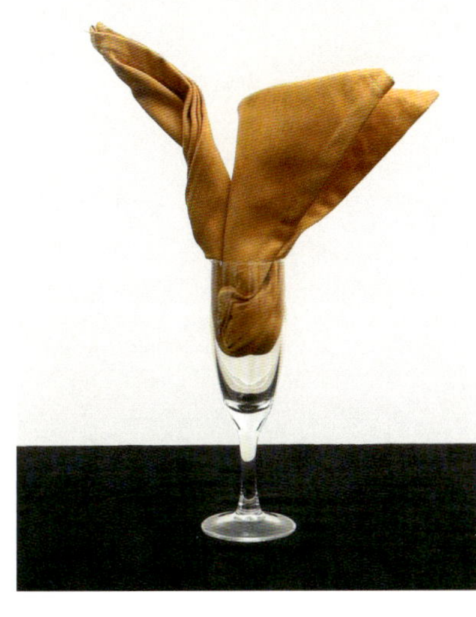
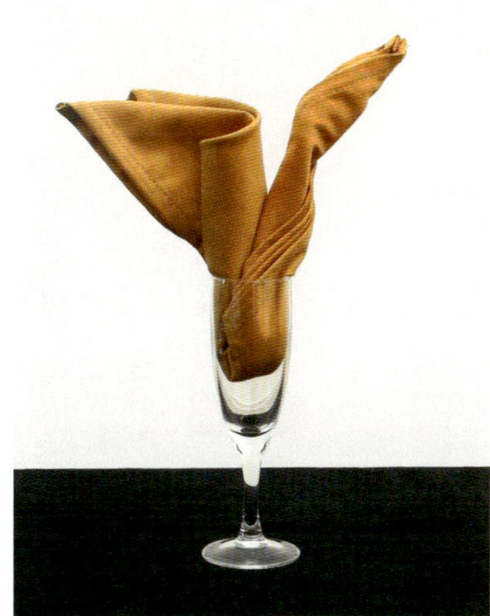

GEORGIA, 2011 (details)

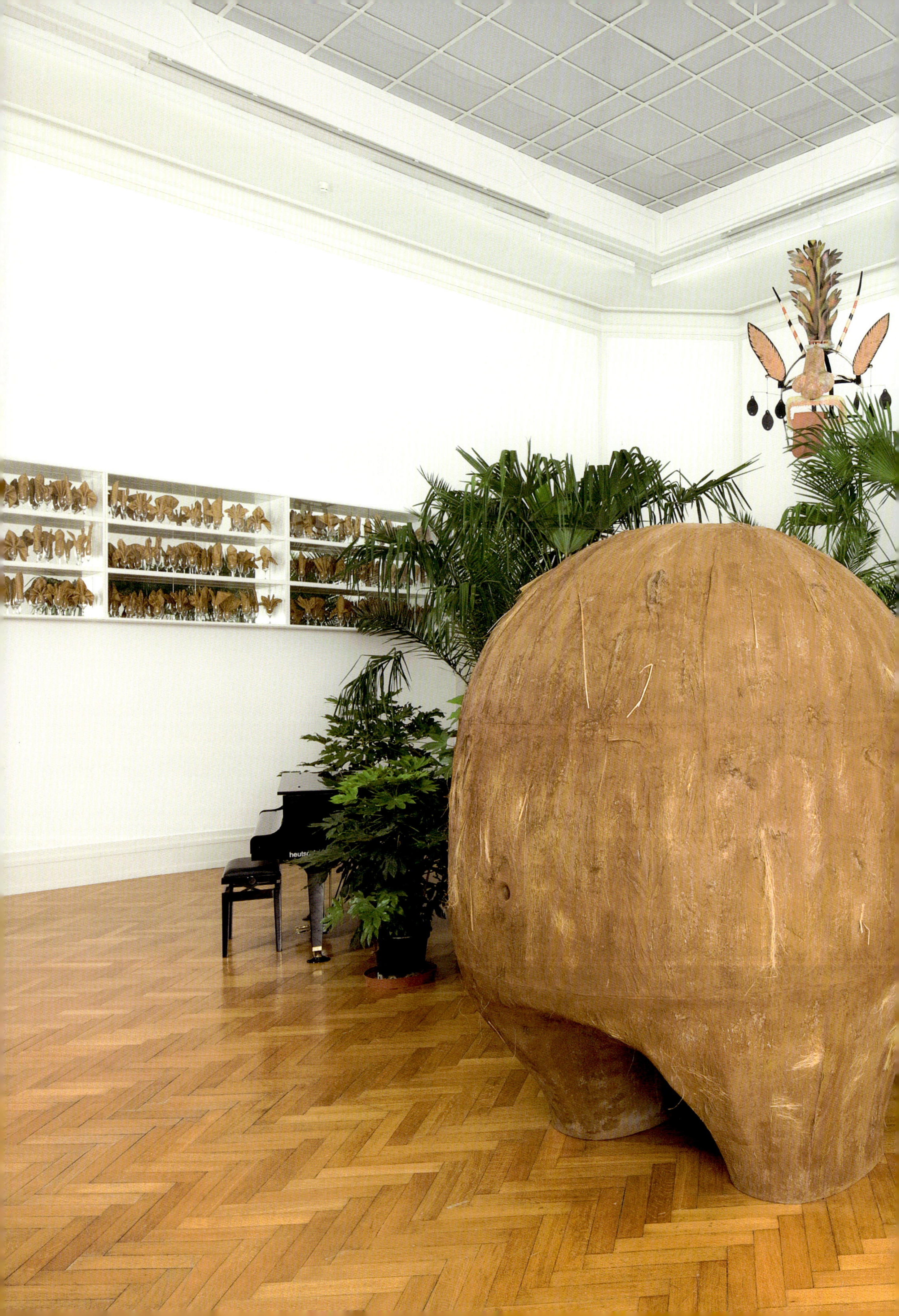

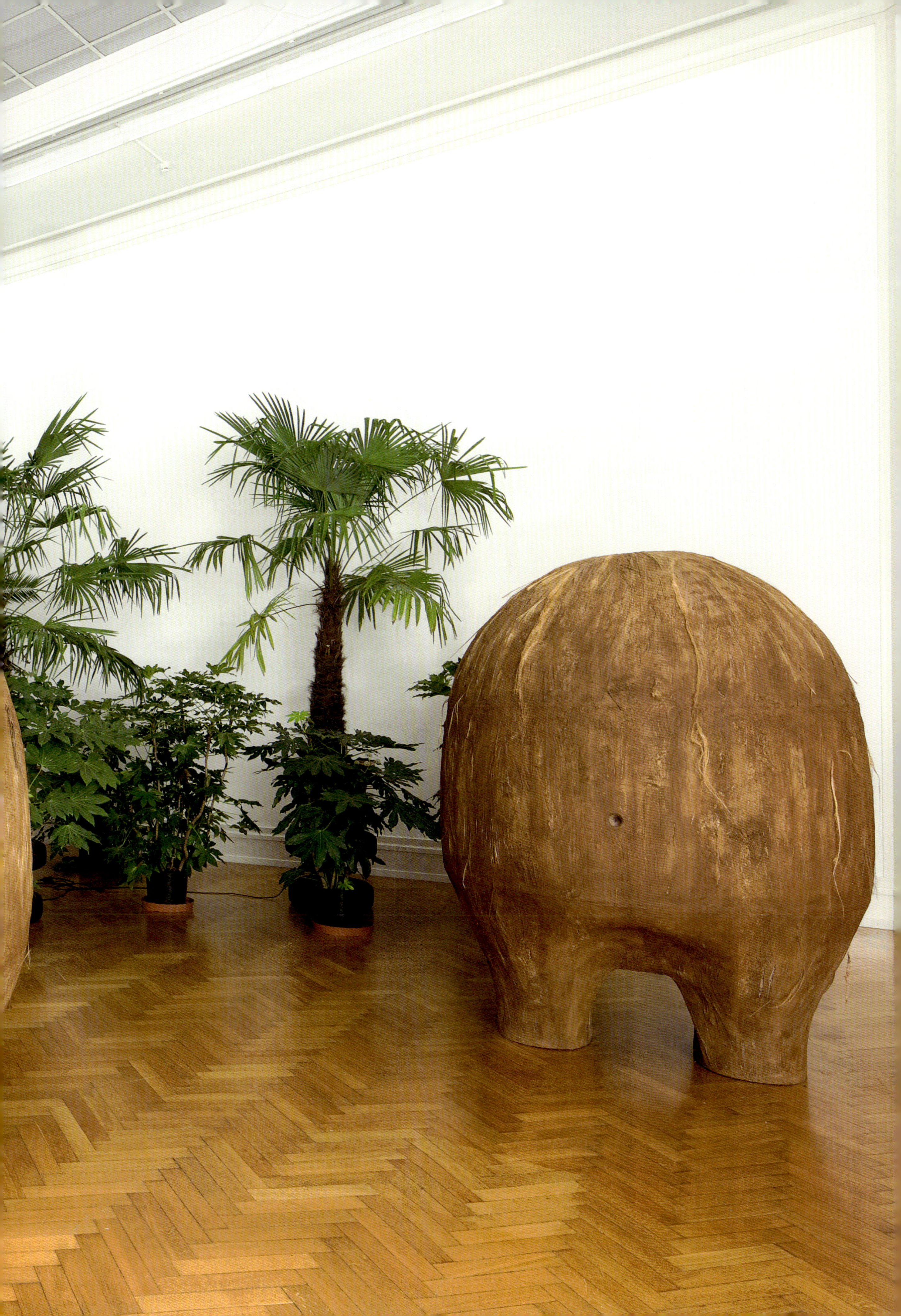

← MALDOROR, 2012, exhibition view, *Baltiques*, Kunsthalle Bern, 2012

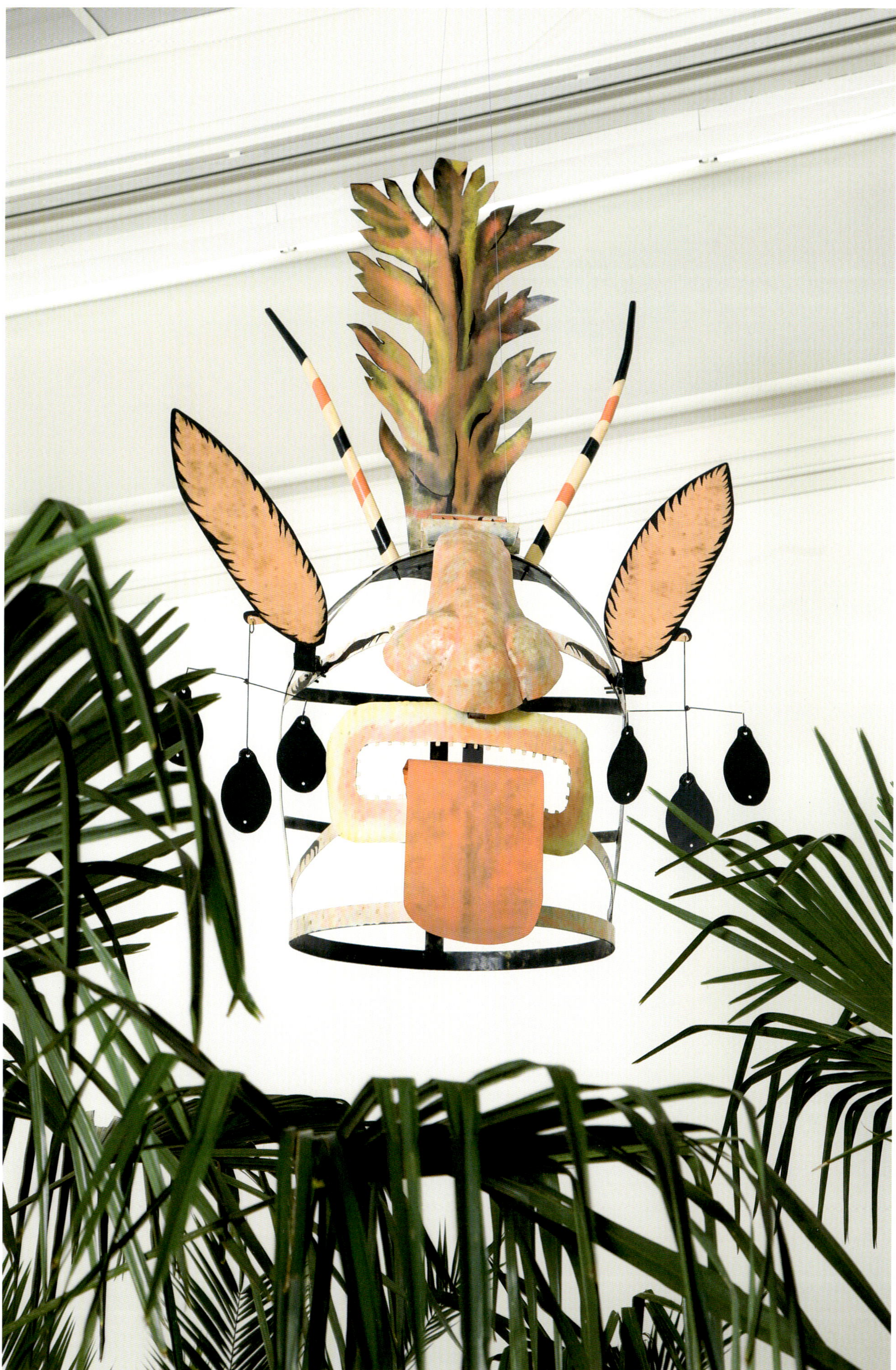

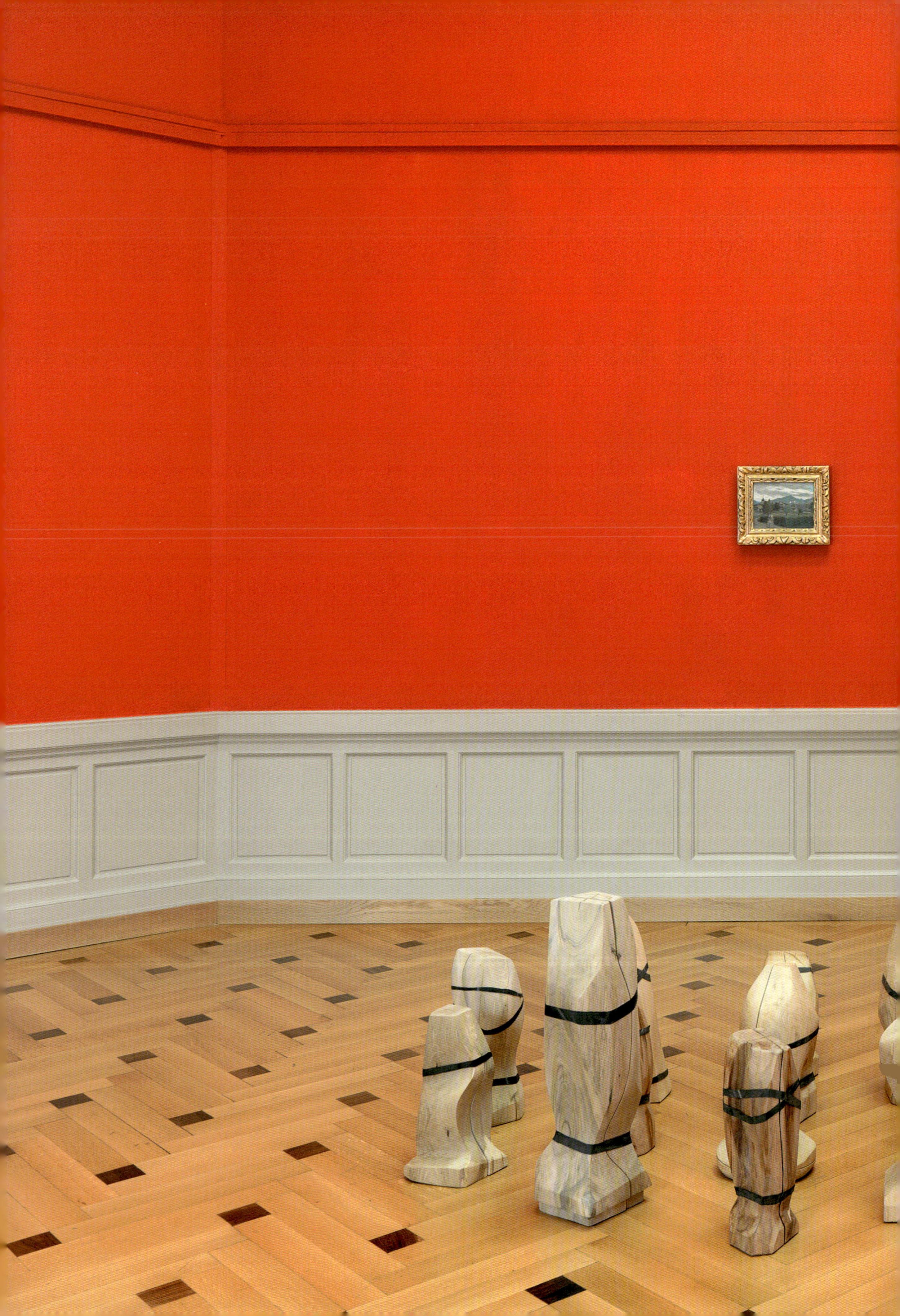

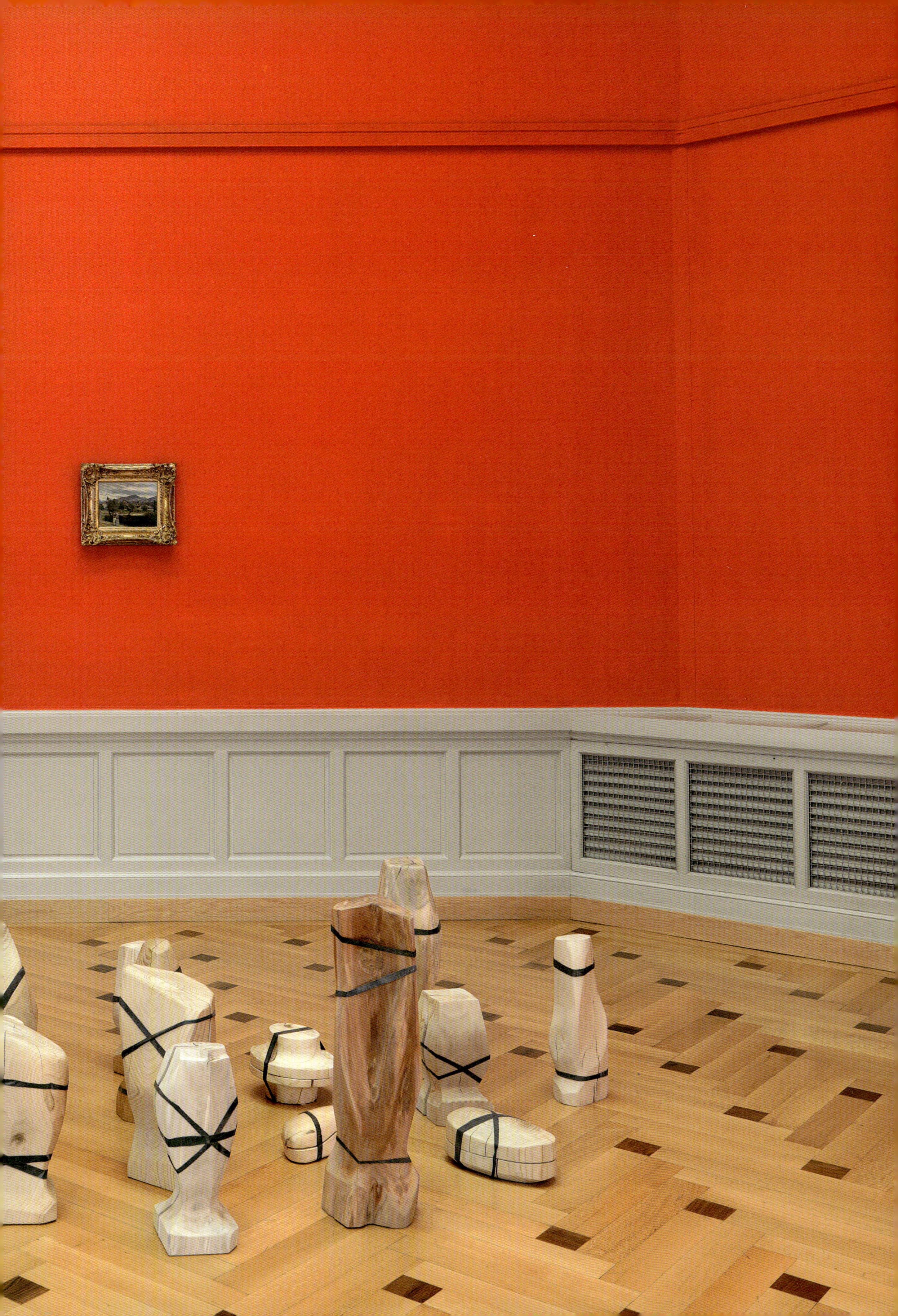

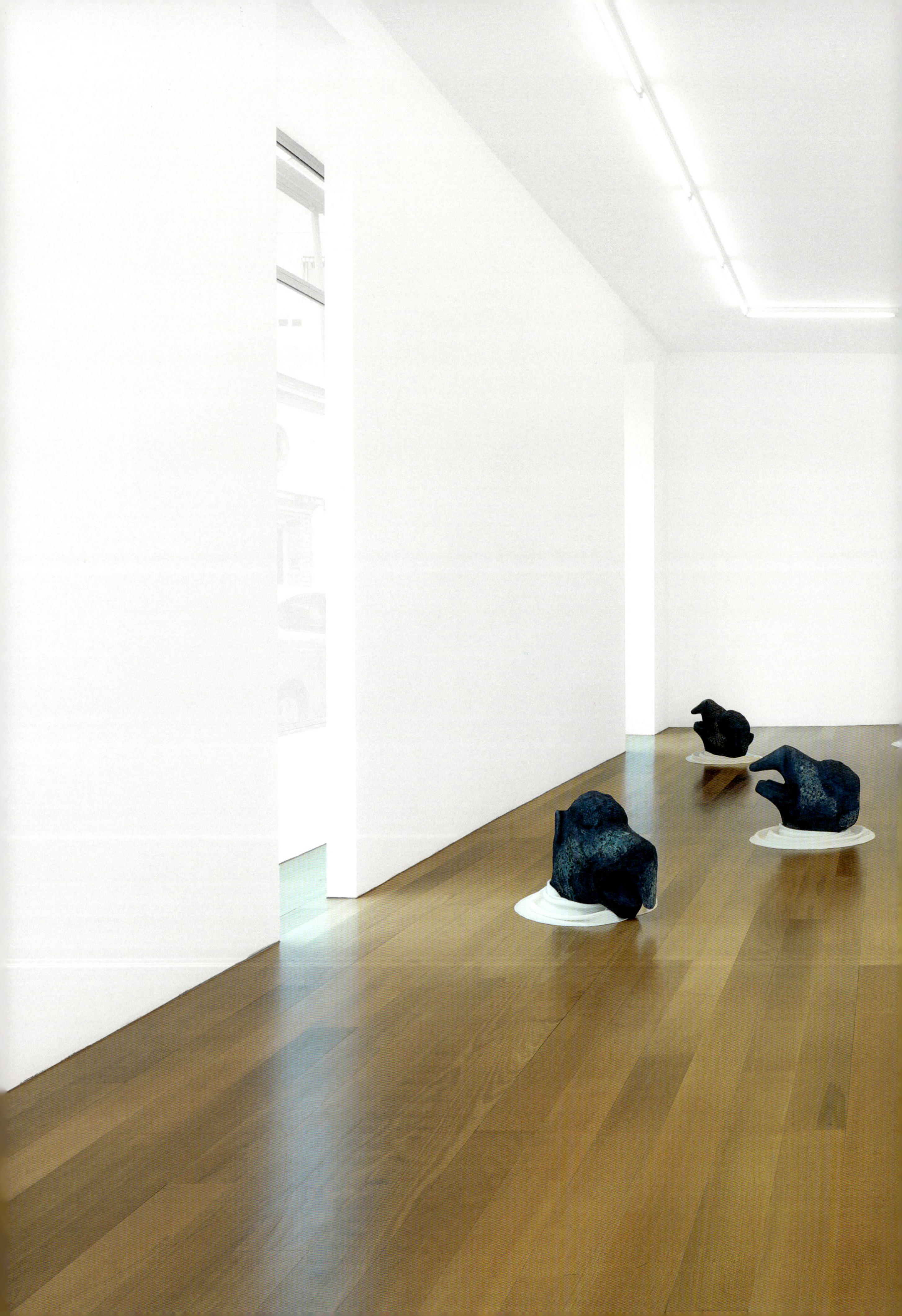

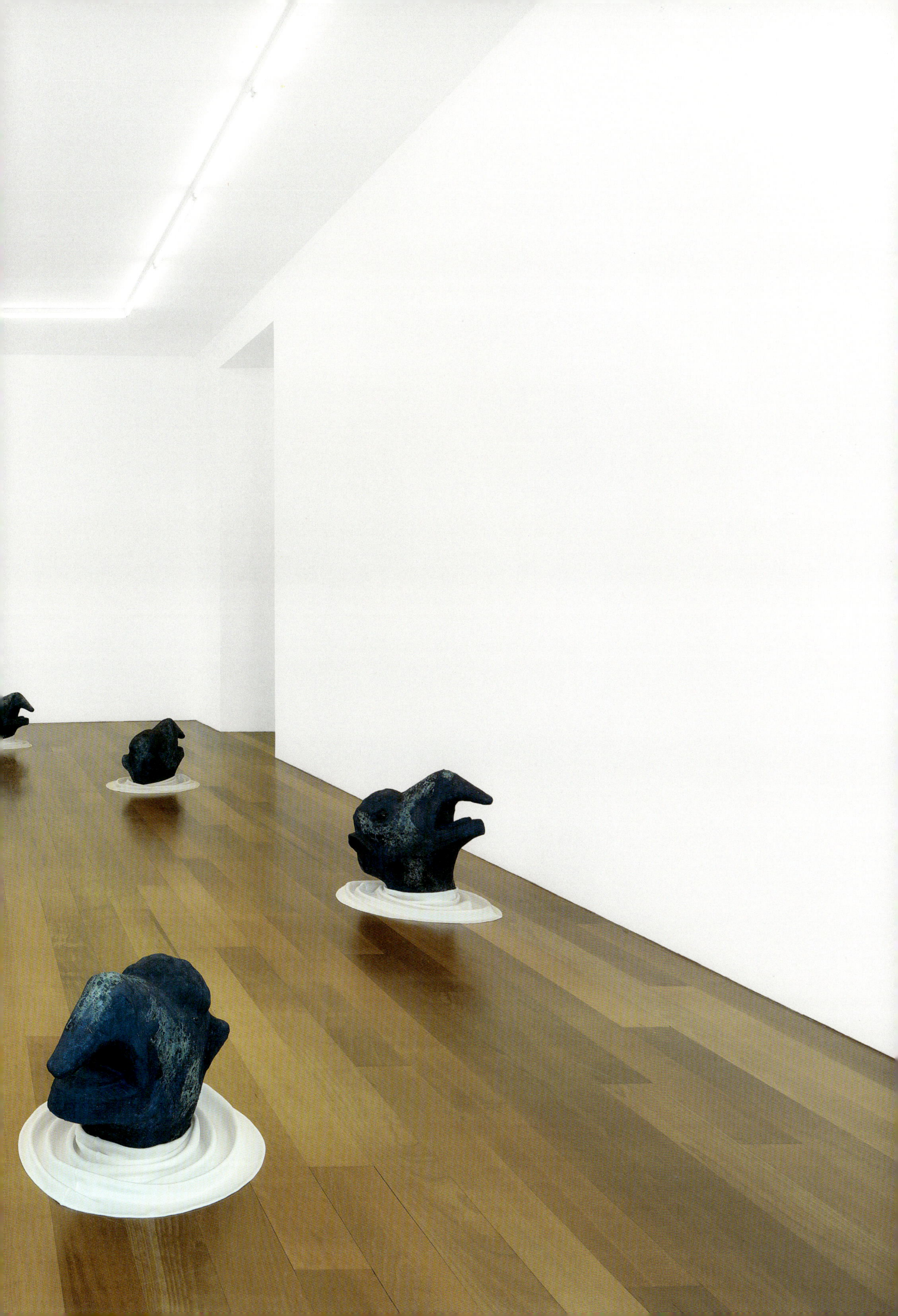

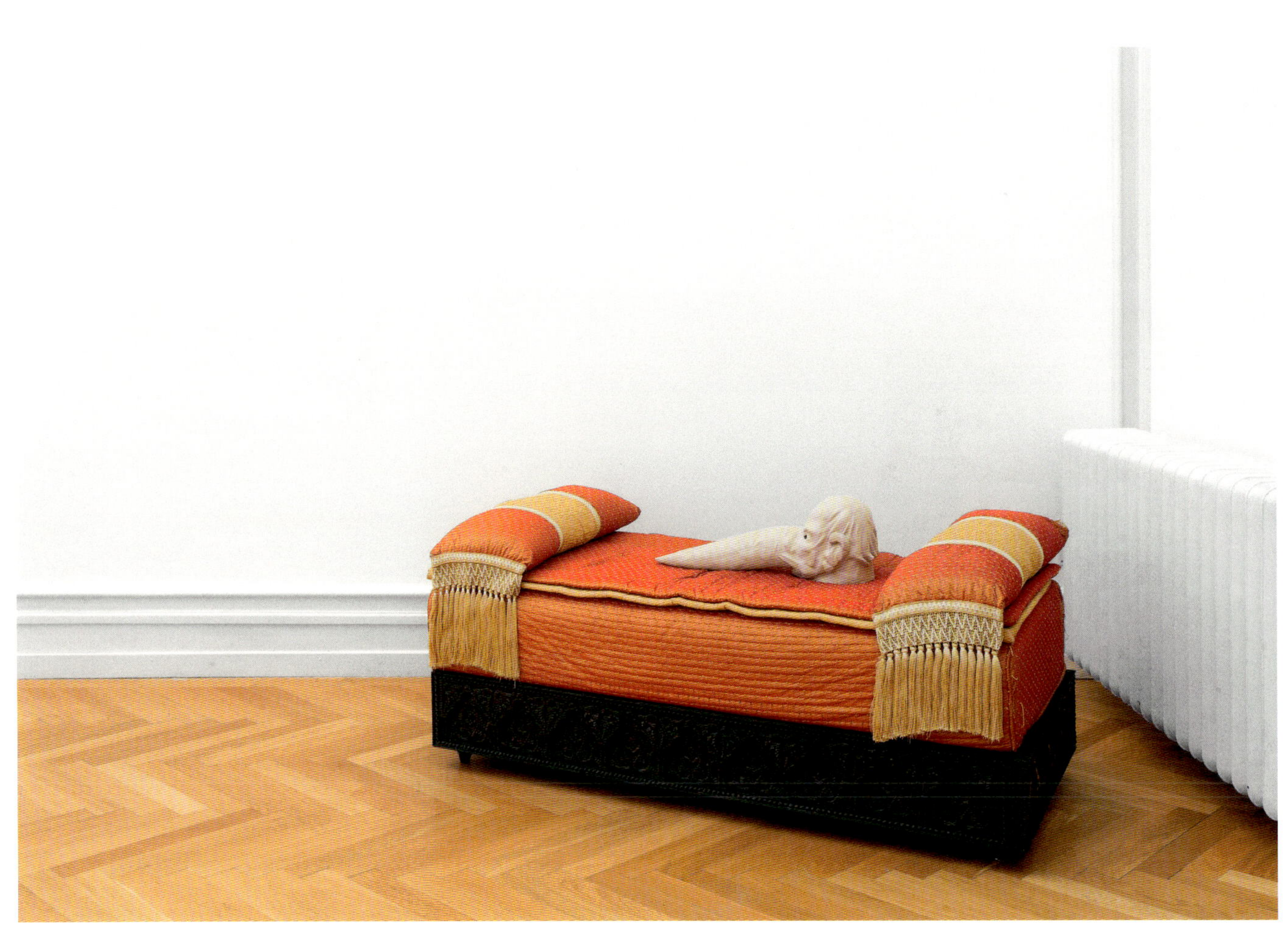

←← LES MANNEQUINS DE COROT: MOULES, 2013, exhibition view, *Les Mannequins de Corot*, Musée d'Art et d'Histoire, Geneva, 2013

← AUGUSTES, 2013, exhibition view, *Denis Savary*, Xippas Art Contemporain, Geneva, 2013

Balconies in the Forest
A Conversation Between Denis Savary and Jean-Yves Jouannais

JEAN-YVES JOUANNAIS Artists recognize one another by the nature of their commitment, the way in which they invent their work. In your case, what strikes me is the way you put yourself into your universe: you shape it by absenting yourself from it. You impose it by disappearing. I think of drowning, of John Keats thinking of the practice of art as drowning, i.e. he didn't understand that artists could have an overview of their subject, be in an overarching, dominating, controlling position. It's below the waterline, when you're drowned by your subject, your obsession, that art starts to be produced, mechanically. A theory that gives a special meaning to the epitaph he had engraved on his tomb: "Here lies one whose name was written in water."

In your work there's this link with drowning, the idea of a man who's drowning. And for that man it's an obsession that he should drown. Now we have to get back to, and dwell on, the etymology of the verb "to obsess." Obsessing a city meant besieging it. In your case, as in mine I think, we're besieged individuals, so we're obsessed by we know not what. When a city is besieged, Paris in 1870 for instance, Parisians knew there were Prussians surrounding it. Our obsessions are rather strange since we exhaust the whole of our lives trying to recognize and identify these things that are besieging and obsessing us.

There you are, that's how I see you proceeding, how I have the impression of picturing you as a man surrounded.

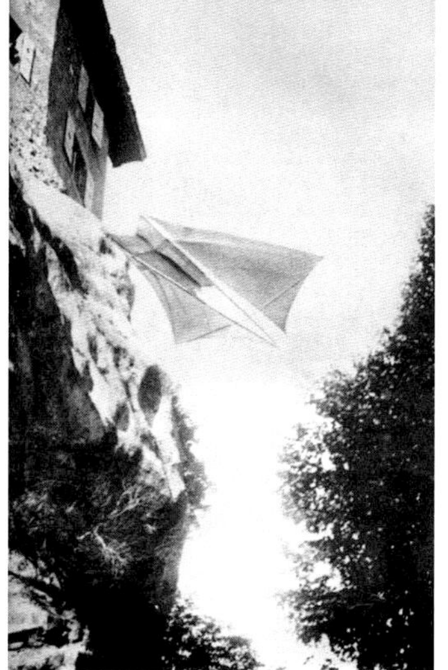

FERDINAND FERBER, 2010
Imprint on micro perforated paper laminated on aluminum, 77 × 120 cm

DENIS SAVARY I made my first films from the windows and surroundings of my family home. I come from the Broye, a region of French-speaking Switzerland that is regularly shrouded in fog. Since my childhood I had the impression that people and landscapes wallowed in a sort of thick, slightly coppery mist, a fog in both the literal and figurative sense— I already used to tell myself lots of stories, even then. Later on, my camera allowed me access to a different reality and let me record all those things. With that tool, I had the sensation of being a stranger, I rediscovered my village and its surroundings. That territory naturally became a sort of playground, a field for exploration. For example, I discovered that it's the region where Captain Ferdinand Ferber used to live, the aviation pioneer who threw himself out of the window of his château several times, trying to escape from earth's gravity by means of his various gliders. Emerging from the mist of the window. Piling up failure upon failure, he only very rarely achieved lift-off with his biplanes, going on to die in 1909 at the age of 47 from the consequences of a plane accident on the ground.

JEAN-YVES JOUANNAIS What interests me, and what I see in your work, is what you describe of your returns, those returns home, to the original mist. How you pull those materials down and bring them back toward a center. We learn, we glean, we discover elements depending on the drift of the exhibitions or discussions. Well, you always go and replant those elements, those discoveries at the center, in the heart. It's like going on journeys, bringing back plant species from them, and replanting them in a garden, yours in this case. There's the idea of spreading out, and simultaneously of going back to the starting point, always ultimately replanting at the center.

But I wanted to go back to the discussion about the liquid element. I see you as someone on a raft. I see you attempting to drown yourself from that raft. And the way you're tempted by drowning has nothing to do with any aspiration to disappear, but is in keeping with a passion of curiosity, an ambition to conquer through non-control. I perceive you more as being like Klaus Kinski in *Aguirre, the Wrath of God* (1972), but less bellicose, more contemplative. Aguirre is on the Amazon River and he remains alone. The drifting raft is overrun by monkeys and he carries on talking about conquest; he tells himself that all these territories on either side of the river effectively belong to him. He sees them, so they are his. He is simply seeking war to validate his conquests. But he's alone, all of his soldiers have died, brought down by illness or Indian arrows. He is forced into contemplation. His violence cannot extend beyond the sphere of his fulminations. You'd be a sort of Swiss conquistador, calmer, more reserved, more melancholic. Anyway that's how you describe yourself when you were endlessly discovering the landscape from your bedroom window. You had fantasies about conquests and they ended up happening. It's in that Swiss landscape that you called on and eventually conjured up oceanic settings, maritime ambiences, and storms such as only the open oceans experience. I like the way you spoke before your *Carrousel* exhibition at the Centre d'art contemporain de La Ferme du Buisson (2010–2011) about that liquid element, how you'd wanted to stress its presence.

DENIS SAVARY At the Centre d'art contemporain de La Ferme du Buisson, the exhibition was surrounded by the noise of the wind and the hot air balloon burners, with a few sounds of instruments here and there. The *Aerolfiades* project consisted of distributing 20 or so street musicians (a "Guggenmusik" or improvised band) across the same number of hot air balloons, the idea being that the piece of music played on the ground should be deconstructed in both a literal and figurative sense when the balloons left the ground one after another. But despite eight attempts in eight consecutive years, it has never been possible to fulfill that film project, due to meteorological conditions. The project was being grafted on to an existing event, at a fixed date in the year. All that exists of that film to date is the soundtrack. Listening to it, you'd think you were a thousand leagues from that little country village near the place where Ferber tried out his gliders; you'd be more inclined to think you were on the beach.

JEAN-YVES JOUANNAIS What's more, that was my impression when I entered the exhibition, before realizing that's what it was.

DENIS SAVARY In one of the exhibition rooms, in the same space, I'd put together a video where you see a man sitting on a bench under a tree, running through his scales on the trumpet (*Brît*, 2004), and I had appended hundreds of drawings to the wall depicting seascapes, done on the pieces of card you find at the end of the packets of papers you use for rolling cigarettes. Surrounded by all these little drawings by Morio (*La Longue route*, 2008–2010), an artist I'd met in Quimper, the trumpet player appeared to be alone on a desert island, and conversely the "droning" sound of his instrument conjured up the signals emitted by a sort of foghorn, like a home port on the open sea.

JEAN-YVES JOUANNAIS There's something else I wanted to say to you. I have a strange passion for dams. I love making dams on rivers, being in a river and spending hours, without speaking, piling up pebbles and creating a fork in the riverbed. It's the story of Agis, King of Sparta, at the siege of Mantinea. Now for me, intervening in the natural flow of a river, with the dream of reversing, or at least redirecting, the course of moving water, has a lot in common with the way we try to reinvent heritages for ourselves.

You're descended from a line whose last representative is your father with whom you imagine a mode of heritage: how he taught you about football, how you talk to him about art. As far as I'm concerned, to create my on-going project *Encyclopédie des guerres* (2008-), I started from my grandfather on my father's side, who died in 1945, and I invented a heritage that ancestor should have passed down to me. I misappropriated the title of a performance by Joseph Beuys to try and express that principle of inventing a heritage for an exhibition: *How to get a dead grandfather to tell you stories about the war*. For me it's all about a dam when you try to change the flow of a river, the course of things, the objective being able to address things to my grandfather while presenting it as if it is he who is passing them on to me. Well, I'm convinced that our activities are comparable, but I don't know what they are. So I tell myself that this idea of building dams, making the flow fork in two, tinkering with modes of heritage to the point of inverting their direction, all that seems to be close to a shared obsession.

DENIS SAVARY What you're saying strikes a chord with me. In the work *Les Mannequins de Corot* (2009), I was interested in Édouard Gaillot, an art historian who specialized in the painter's work and life. By dint of working on his subject, he ended up seeing Corots everywhere and fantasizing about hidden works by the painter, works attributed to other artists. In order to justify his research, he started looking for evidence that would validate its veracity. The proof he sought was the painter's signature, which he divined and ended up seeing on works more or less everywhere, in particular on reproductions of paintings in general books about art history. When he discovered these "invisible" signatures, he circled them in pencil or pen, and in the end it looked like a bite out of the folds of a Watteau, a mischievous presence in the corner of the lips of a Madonna by Titian, tattoos on the body of a prehistoric Venus. I like the way people, when they nurture an obsession, end up twisting reality, tinkering with history. Édouard Gaillot credited Corot with qualities that go well beyond the painter's capabilities, in particular an ability to travel through time.

At the Musée des Augustins in Toulouse, for the 2009 Printemps de Septembre, I presented the actor Serge Renko, getting him to act out the role of a specialist on Camille Corot, a disciple of the historian Gaillot. To do so I "loaded" him with information about Gaillot's study project so that he would tell that story back to me, then "released" him in the monumental staircase of the museum. He spoke about the works as if they were Corots; it was lovely to see him performing on that staircase, amid all those sculptures, to end up astride *Le Cauchemar* (1894) by Eugène Thivier, looking for a signature.

JEAN-YVES JOUANNAIS That conjures up in my mind what you try to do with the dancer and choreographer Delphine Lorenzo, something I'm tempted by too. During a lecture at the Comédie theater in Reims, I felt I was mediocre. My speech lacked fluidity. What I was able to say there was perhaps no more and no less interesting than it was at other times, but I didn't find any graciousness in that speech. Afterward I told myself that what I was after wasn't so much interesting ideas as a plastic quality suitable for linking those ideas. Like people who go rock-climbing without worrying about the speed of the ascent, but more about the greater or lesser harmony, the fluidity of their progress, of the holds and pull-ups. Gesture rather than a corpus, a choreography by way of thought. It seems to me that it's the same thing for you. To be sure, you produce objects, but we have an intuition that it's a bit contrived and forced. In any case, there's a temptation toward something else. That harmony, that fluidity, that adaptability in the sequence of thoughts, dreams, has more to do with a climatological creation. You attempt to control, to design a meteorology, and I think that the term "fluidity" used to describe the economy of rivers, springs, fountains—since there are some in your videos and your exhibitions—was more there to represent what basically interested us, namely the fluidity of gestures. You're a dancer. A rather awkward, rather impeded dancer who's trying very quietly to be independent ...

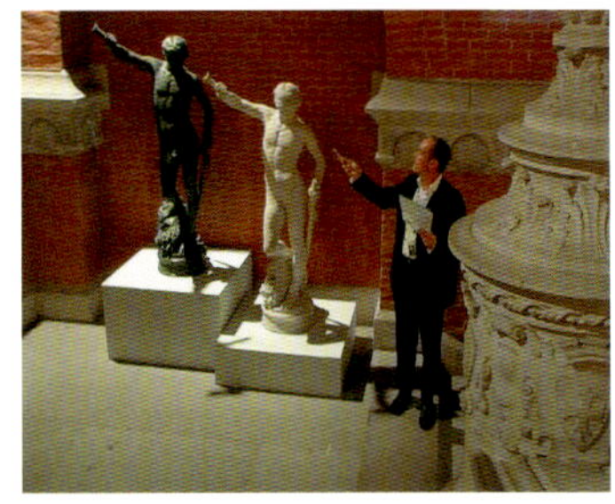

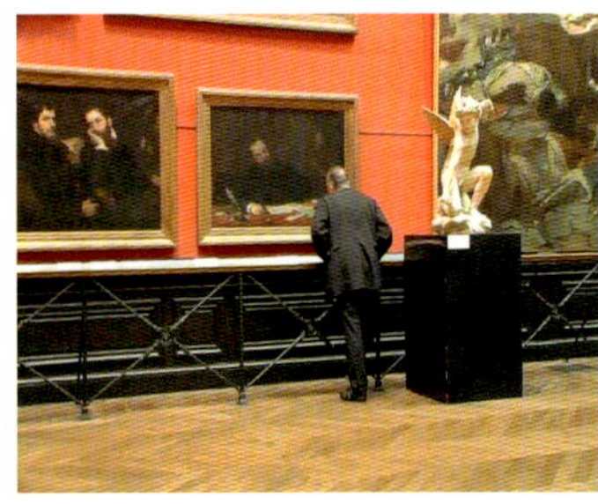

LES MANNEQUINS DE COROT, 2009
With Serge Renko, actor, and Delphine Lorenzo, choreographer
Performance view, Le Printemps de Septembre, Musée des Augustins, Toulouse, 2009

DENIS SAVARY There's an anecdote told to me by my father, a former football coach. His team was losing. The players couldn't manage to get it together, to find themselves on the pitch; everyone was strung up and tense. At halftime, despondent, they all went back to the dressing room to hear my father's instructions. But he didn't say a word. All he did was put out the lights and turn on the showers for the entire duration of the break, leaving the players alone in the dark. When the whistle blew, he switched the lights back on. The players, as if they'd been revitalized, went onto the pitch and ended up winning the game, reversing the course of the match. I've always really liked that story. Something strange happened in the dressing room at halftime, and I thought I had spotted that thing in dance, hence my desire to work with Delphine Lorenzo.

I think that what interests me is when the elements exist neither as such nor exclusively in the connection. It's as if it were a question through the very act, that of establishing a relationship between two things, of designating a specific type of presence that is in both cases associated with an absence.

JEAN-YVES JOUANNAIS I understand. In what I see of your practice, there are forms making marks that are evolving. There's nothing definitive about them. It's easier to grasp that idea if you consider the famous painting made by Turner in 1812, *Snow Storm: Hannibal and His Army Crossing the Alps*. Two years earlier, while visiting friends in Wales, he was walking in the hills when he was overtaken by a huge storm. He only had an envelope with him, which he used to make a sketch. He wanted to record a meteorological phenomenon that impressed him, a truly picturesque landscape, i.e. in his view worthy of being conveyed in a painting. That sketch depicting a storm would become *Snow Storm: Hannibal Crossing the Alps* two years later. What came first was the recording of a climatological phenomenon. And then Turner must have said to himself that the storm itself perhaps wasn't satisfactory, i.e. adequate as a subject. If a picture aspired to go down in the history of art, it had to be a history painting, therefore a picture of war. So we don't see Hannibal, we don't see the elephants, we see nothing, but its title turns it into a very enigmatic object. Let's suppose he could have painted just one single canvas, and throughout his life could have given it every possible conceivable title, going right through them. What's more, you did the same thing when you installed the work *Le Must* (2004; 2008–2010) at the Centre d'art contemporain de La Ferme du Buisson in a completely different way from how you first did it. The video became a lighting system. Five or twenty years from now we'll perhaps find it again somewhere else, in a different exhibition, with a different title, a different function.

DENIS SAVARY I think that what I particularly value in works is their capacity never to be closed. They have the ability to move, to say something else, they have a life of their own. For my first exhibition at La Russille in Switzerland in 2005, I had this sentence in my head: "Elles portent des plaisirs qui leur sont propres mais qui n'ont rien à voir avec le plaisir de se gratter." [They bring pleasures all of their own that have nothing to do with the pleasure of scratching oneself.] I think Calder said it. It became the title of my exhibition. I like the idea that a work should remain incomprehensible, as if it is in its nature continually to escape any definition. So it's important in my work that the way objects are perceived shouldn't be determined. It all evolves to keep rhythm with encounters. Essentially, there's an unknown quotient, and that's what's really exciting, I think.

JEAN-YVES JOUANNAIS I do in fact think there's something of that nature: not knowing why we do this or that, knowing that people are not going to understand from the outside why we do it, because we ourselves don't know what it is. And I think that when it comes down to it, that activity makes it possible to measure time. In measuring that time, objects are collected, brought together. But they're very secondary in relation to what we have in our heads. It's a poetic ambition that can't be reduced to all these marks. In these undertakings, this way of working, there is simultaneously great modesty and huge ambition.

DENIS SAVARY I think that one of the mysteries of our practices is that they hold together. We don't know why. Like a castle made of cardboard that turns out to be of brick. I'm thinking of those crazy projects by architects of hollow spaces, the master builders of Ajanta, designing plans for those underground multi-story dwellings, abraded out of a monolith. Those temples weren't built. They were just unblocked, if not cleared, or rather set free by bringing air into the solid rock, by a generation of miners who were also engineers and sculptors.

Our great ambition would be to leave people perplexed, but to induce a sort of enthusiastic perplexity in them, by offering them something that seems essential to us.

JEAN-YVES JOUANNAIS What's important is that we spend our time waiting for that essential thing. For me, this question of waiting is very present in your work: the nails waiting for objects, your portable furniture waiting for a purpose, the way in which you film, always on the lookout. This troubles me a lot. With the *Encyclopédie des guerres*, I think I'm looking for a precise object that is apparently the source of all my emotions, and I thought I'd spotted it at a certain moment in a text, in an image. What overwhelms me today is this business of waiting. It's neither war, nor death, but this warrior-like stance during the "phony war," as attested to by *Un balcon en forêt* (1958, *A Balcony in the Forest*) by Julien Gracq, or *Il deserto dei Tartari* (1940, *The Tartar Steppe*) by Dino Buzzati. Grange and Drogo are both waiting for History to show up. What's amusing is that *Il deserto dei Tartari* was translated in 1949 in France. Then Beckett wrote *Waiting for Godot*. Well, Godot, Drogo, there can be no doubt that it's the same name. And that the reason why Godot can't arrive on Beckett's stage is because he's waiting for the war at the Fort Bastiani of *Il deserto dei Tartari*.

This question of waiting, this wait for the resolution of an obsession, the crystallization of a passion, we'll be waiting for it till the end of our days. Nonetheless, this doesn't mean it's a matter of wasting time. We have to invent ourselves, try to justify our existence on earth. Does this strike a chord with you, this question of waiting?

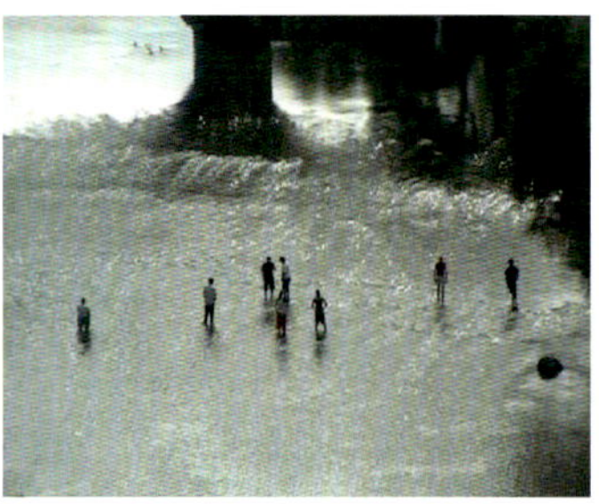

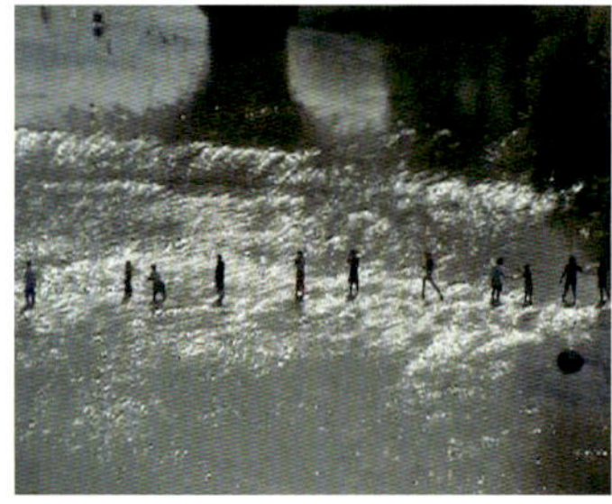

BELVÉDÈRE, 2005
Video, color, sound, 12'50"
Collection Mamco, Geneva

DENIS SAVARY When I came across that guy playing the trumpet in the middle of the countryside (filmed in the video *Brît*), my original intention had been to leave the house and go and film a particularly sophisticated watering system in the fields across from where I live. Then I was disturbed by a sound I heard in the distance, like a droning noise. I walked for a little until I found this musician sitting alone on a bench. At the time I had the strange impression that it was the trumpeter who was peacefully waiting for me there, sitting under a tree. There was no need to look for him, he was already there.

We were talking about choreography. I find my video *Belvédère* (2005), which I filmed from the terrace of a café by the same name in Fribourg, remarkable from a choreographic point of view: the movements of the people in the river who are splashing one another and gradually forming a dam to collect things that are coming down from higher up. It's hard to imagine such a scene; the things are there, it's just a question of spotting them, like the small floating things that arrive with the current and end up being fished out, or not.

JEAN-YVES JOUANNAIS I see. I regularly make an endeavor to picture the *Encyclopédie des guerres* in my mind. At one time I saw it as a sort of bath. I saw a receptacle where I piled up scraps of texts, scraps of images, so that after several years I'd be in a position to dive into it physically and feel very concretely in contact with all the trumpetings of Hannibal's elephants, all the shots fired at every epoch, all the shouts in all the deserts, all the rubble of all the cities, all the sighs of all the wounded on the fields of all the battles, and be simultaneously in physical contact with that reality.

DENIS SAVARY That makes me think of *The Ocean Wave* (1899), a book by Ambrose Bierce. Following a shipwreck, the character is prompted to fashion a raft for himself with things that had previously been thrown overboard. Strangely enough, and contrary to all expectations, the raft floats.

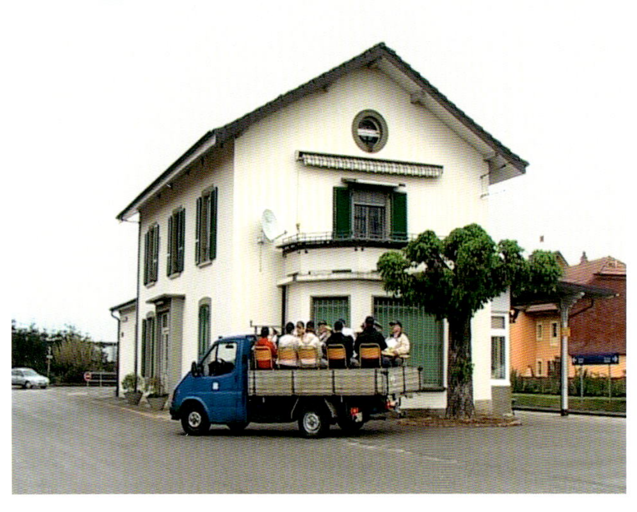

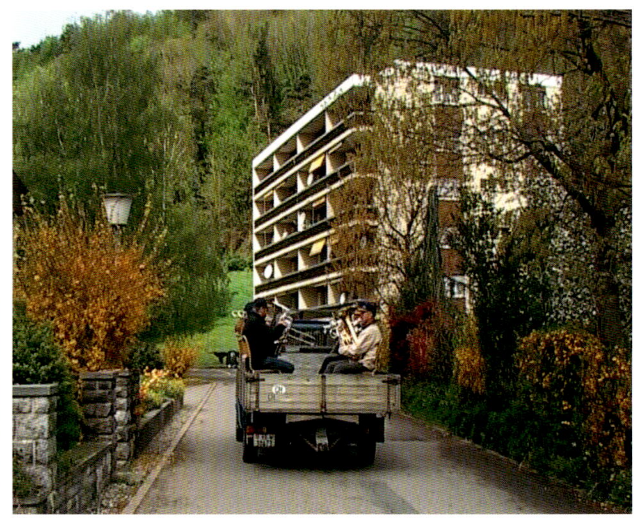

LA DIANE, 2004
Video, color, sound, 13'52"
Collection Mamco, Geneva

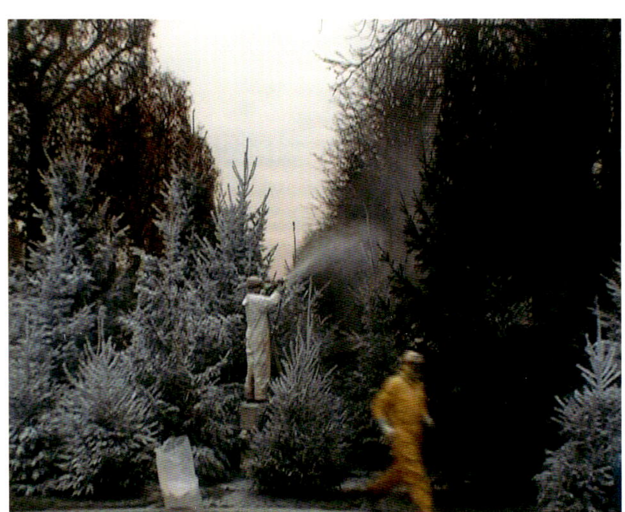

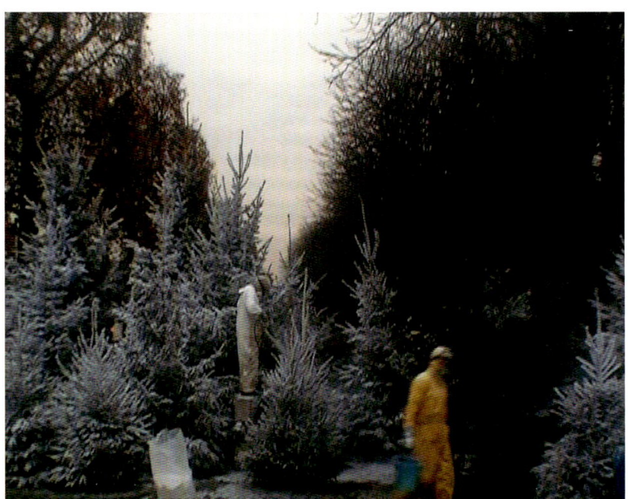

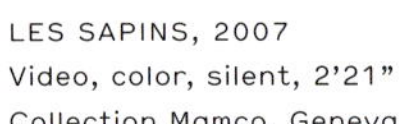

LES SAPINS, 2007
Video, color, silent, 2'21"
Collection Mamco, Geneva

The Savary Pastorale

Philippe-Alain Michaud

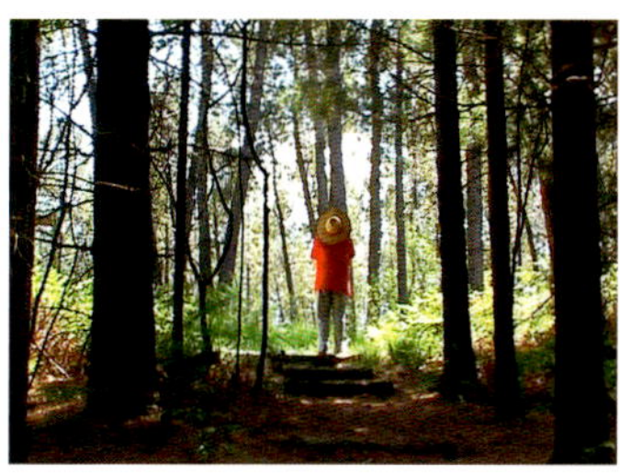

LE FRAU, 2006
Video, color, sound, 10'21"
Collection Mamco, Geneva

Sheepfolds, properly speaking, are paintings from the golden age put within human reach, and stripped of all the marvelous hyperbole with which poets have laden their description. It is the reign of freedom, innocent pleasures, peace, these goods for which human beings feel they were born when their passions leave them a few moments of silence in which to recognize themselves. In short, they are the convenient, joyful retreat of a man who has a simple yet sensitive heart and has found the means of making that happy century return for him.
— Denis Diderot and Jean d'Alembert, *Encyclopédie* or *Dictionnaire raisonné des sciences, des arts et des métiers,* Paris 1751 and 1772, entry on "Pastorale"

Still shots, generalized use of sequential shots, a single action in real time, familiar circumscribed places—except for some exotic excursions—at the perimeter of the Canton of Vaud, precisely in the village of Granges-Marnand and its immediate vicinity: Denis Savary's films are made according to formal principles of unremitting austerity that contrast with their slightly bizarre, or even openly frenzied character. Everything conspires to understate the importance of the subject represented, to reduce the film to an indissociably euphoric and depressing minimal diegesis, which makes the effect the artist is systematically seeking operate all the more in the image, an effect that could be called, giving the term back its etymological force, an effect of fantasy. It is a question of isolating an incidental and decontextualized action in a motionless frame and stretching out of shot, in order to turn the very insignificance into an event, and the image into a place in which to exercise the imagination.

In 2004 in *Brît*, in a rural setting bathed in the golden light of a late summer afternoon, Denis Savary recorded the image of a young man lolling on a bench under a tree, its circular foliage filling the whole upper part of the frame. The young man is playing a trumpet (off key), trying to drag a few tired scales out of it. The film seems like a visual reminiscence, mildly tinged with irony, of the beginning of the first eclogue of Virgil's *Bucolics*:

> Tityre, tu patulae recubans sub tegmine fagi
> Silvestrem tenui musam meditaris avena,

translated in verse by Henry Wadsworth Longfellow in 1893:

> Tityrus, thou in the shade of a spreading beech tree reclining
> Meditatest, with slender pipe, the Muse of the woodlands,[1]

and in prose by J.W. Mackail in 1899: "Tityrus, thou where thou liest under the covert of spreading beech, broodest on thy slim pipe over the Muse of the woodland ... "[2]

1
English translation by Henry Wadsworth Longfellow, "Virgil's First Eclogue," in *Complete Poetical Works,* ed. Horace E. Scudder, Houghton, Mifflin & Co., Boston and New York 1893.

2
"Eclogue I: Tityrus," *The Eclogues of Virgil*, trans. J. W. MacKail, T.B. Mosher, Portland, Maine 1899.

However, the reference that gives the film its mythological background, and seems to make it timeless and remove it from the strict immanence of what the image circumscribes is not only literary: the stationary moped that makes a red splash in the landscape on the right of the tree, and on the left, in the foreground, the stone drinking trough, are unequivocally reminiscent of the composition of *The Pastoral Concert* by Titian (c. 1509, Paris, Musée du Louvre). At the center of the picture, a naked nymph is playing the flute in front of two men sitting on the ground, one of whom is wearing a red hat, while a second nymph, on the left, is pouring water into a fountain. In the manner of the Titian painting whose composition he adopts to turn it into a sort of tableau vivant, Denis Savary treats the landscape in musical terms, playing on the resonances between its contrasts, its convolutions, its color harmonies and the rhythms, melodies, and chords of the music, which he transforms into dissonances and lulls: no longer an allegory of poetry contrasting or associating the perceptible with the intelligible, but its realistic version, through its inscription in the boredom of a summer afternoon.

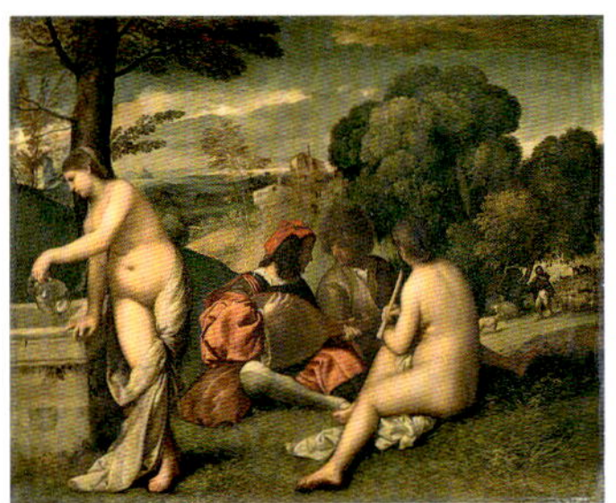

Titian
THE PASTORAL CONCERT, C. 1509
Paris, Musée du Louvre

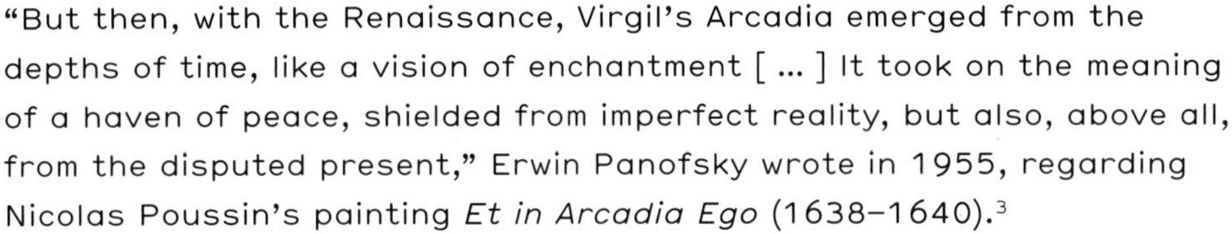

"But then, with the Renaissance, Virgil's Arcadia emerged from the depths of time, like a vision of enchantment [...] It took on the meaning of a haven of peace, shielded from imperfect reality, but also, above all, from the disputed present," Erwin Panofsky wrote in 1955, regarding Nicolas Poussin's painting *Et in Arcadia Ego* (1638–1640).[3]

Denis Savary's disillusioned Arcadia likewise functions as a way of conjuring up historical time: it transposes the Neoplatonic doctrine of the imagination onto a discretely parodic level, a doctrine that sees the visible world as an imitation of the world of ideas, the parody also being that of the iconographic interpretation of the picture.[4] We find the same anachronistic and deceptive device in *La Courtisane* (2003): sitting on a bistro chair, with his back turned to the camera's lens, a young musician plays the hurdy-gurdy, the emblematic instrument of the pastorale,[5] opposite a gravel pit with roaring motocross bikes going up and down in it. The angry noise of the engines mingles with that of the instrument, while the circuits performed by the bikes echo the circular movements of the hand activating the handle of the instrument: here again, in the noise and dust of this sublunar world, the film repeats the movement of the spheres, with the bard on the hurdy-gurdy seemingly celebrating its inaccessible harmony.

Denis Savary stages the irruption of fable into everyday life in the shape of a disillusionment that in turn becomes magical. His films inscribe an idyllic vision into a prosaic setting that simultaneously renders it opaque and reveals it. That ambiguity is perceptible even in the titles of the pieces: *La Courtisane* is the name of a courtly dance, just as *La Diane* (2004) is not only the name of a car, but of the goddess of hunting, to whom the piece, played in the early hours in deserted villages by the Granges-Marnand band installed on the back of a pick-up truck, seems to be dedicated.

In Denis Savary's films, as in the pastoral, the music, or rather the travesty of it, plays a crucial role: in *Le Must* (2004), beams of colored light sweep across the deserted dance floor of a nightclub to the sound of disco music that is being played for nobody; in *Le Facteur d'orgue* (2004),

3
Erwin Panofsky, "Et in Arcadia ego: Poussin and the Elegiac Tradition," *Meaning in the Visual Arts. Views from the Outside*, Institute for Advanced Study, Princeton 1995.

4
For the iconography of *The Pastoral Concert*, see Erwin Panofsky, *Problems in Titian, Mostly Iconographic*, New York University Press, New York 1969.

5
Paul Fustier, "La vielle villageoise: un signifiant du mythe de l'Arcadie," http://paul.fustier.pagesperso-orange.fr (last accessed September 2013)

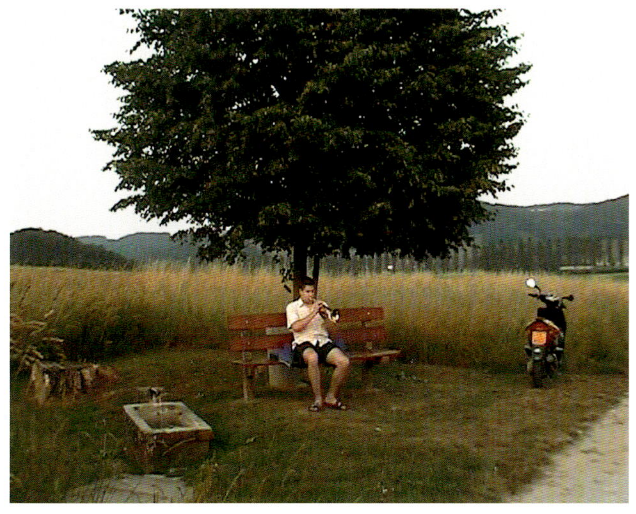

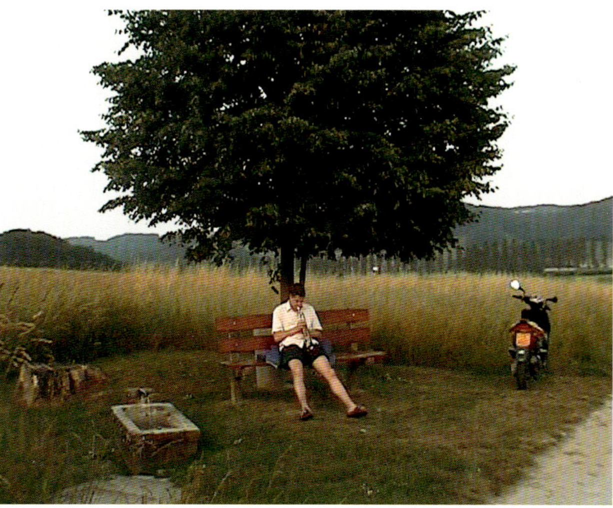

BRÎT, 2004
Video, color, sound, 6'09"
Collection Mamco, Geneva

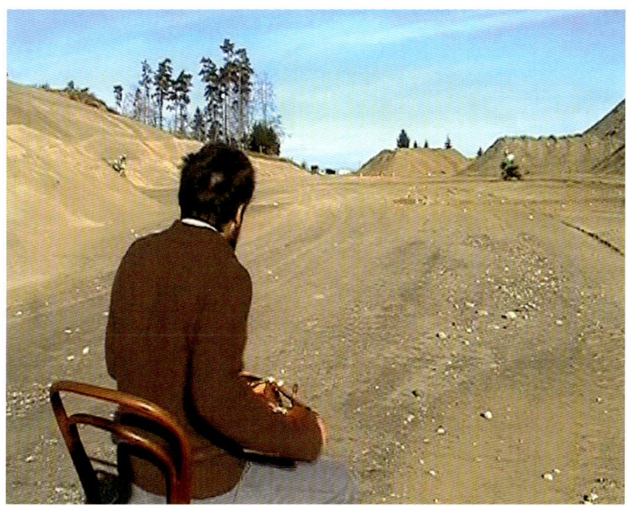

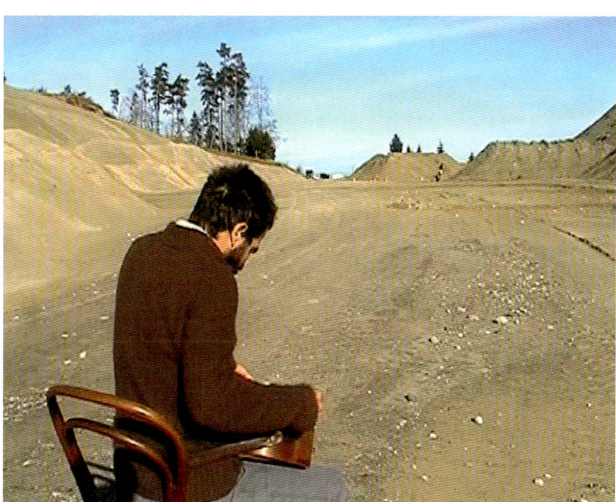

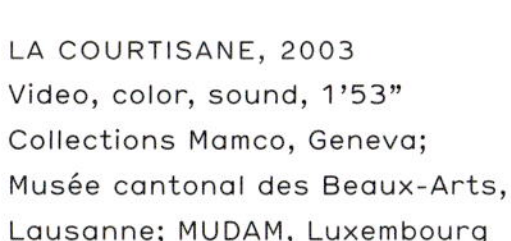

LA COURTISANE, 2003
Video, color, sound, 1'53"
Collections Mamco, Geneva;
Musée cantonal des Beaux-Arts,
Lausanne; MUDAM, Luxembourg

in the empty setting of a modern church, throughout an interminable 20-minute still shot, we hear a sort of musical stuttering, the tuning of the grand organ which assumes an anachronistic presence in this concrete decor. Thus through the stretching of time and inaction it is a question of staging that form of melancholy torpor the Christian tradition called "acedia." Giorgio Agamben describes its effect in these terms: "Fixed in the scandalous contemplation of a goal that reveals itself in the act by which it is precluded and that it is therefore so much more obsessive to the degree that it becomes unattainable, the *acidiosus* (slothful one) finds himself or herself in a paradoxical position in which, as in Kafka's aphorism, 'There exists a point of arrival, but no path,' and there is no escape because one cannot flee from what cannot even be reached."[6]

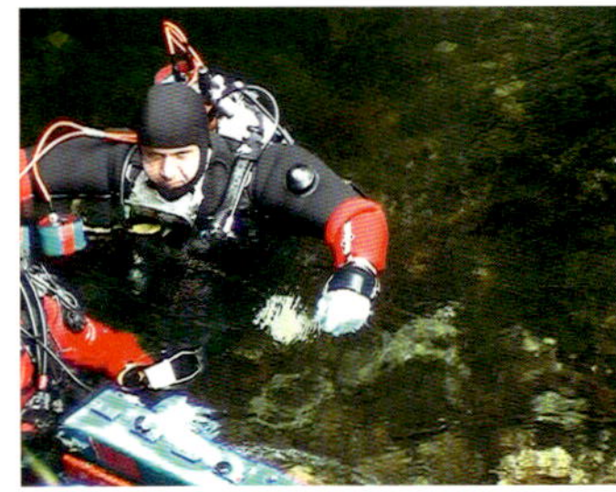

CLAUDE, 2006
Video, color, silent, 7'22"
Collection Mamco, Geneva

6
Giorgio Agamben, *Stanzas: The Word and the Phantasm in Western Culture*, trans. Ronald L. Martinez, University of Minnesota, Minneapolis 1992, p. 6.

This is how Savary redefines film as a structure of pure waiting within which his figures turn up like ludicrous, unreal ghosts. The androgynous silhouette that appears, motionless, as if petrified, in the clearing in *Le Frau* (2006), a circular hat taking the place of a face, has lost its unique identity—it has no features, we do not know if we are looking at the back or the front—but also its generic identity ("le Frau" is both a forest in Le Quercy and a German word meaning woman, here declined with a masculine definite article); the cataleptic body of the sleeping boy in *Rumine* (2007), whose striped vest merges mimetically into the steps across which he is sprawled, occupies the center of the composition, while fleeting shadows move past, confined to the edges of the image. Claude, dressed in his frogman's suit, floats in the black water of the Vallorbe caves, lost in limbo, like an amphibious ectoplasm (*Claude*, 2006); the extras in *Rôlistes* (2005), dressed in furs and medieval costumes, surround a 4 × 4 broken down in the forest as if they had emerged from a Walter Scott novel, transforming role play into a ghost story; the lamentable performance of *Les Charlots* (2005), dressed up as cabaret majorettes, performing their failed act on the stage of a makeshift theater in front of a tropical-themed backdrop, is no longer anything more than the choreographic reminder of order and beauty, signaling both their absence and their reality.

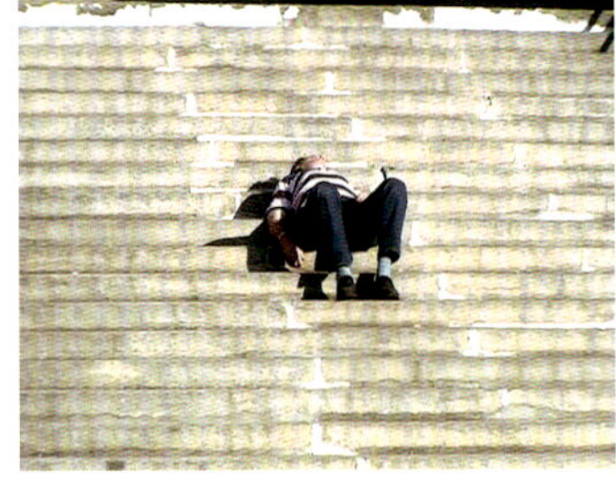

RUMINE, 2007
Video, color, silent, 6'38"
Collection Mamco, Geneva

These specters dress up, make a noise, make music, but they do not speak: absent to others and themselves alike, they are extras at a sad party celebrating an elegiac world whose lost harmony they can only imitate. To describe Savary's filmed works, we could take the words of Faribole in *Coelina ou l'enfant du mystère*, the pastoral play in three acts by René Charles Guibert de Pixerécourt, "in prose and very spectacular," first shown on the stage of the Ambigu-Comique on 15 Fructidor of year VIII. Addressing three peasants playing the tambourine, the musette and the accordion and dancing on a bench—the play is set in Savoie—he says: "À present ... Placez-vous pour la danse ... ohé ... La musique ... Bon ... Voilà la place de l'orchestre ... Grimpez là dessus ... Et vive la joie." [Now ... Take your places for the dance ... Heigh ho ... The musicians ... Good ... Here's where the band goes ... Right ... Climb up here ... And long live happiness.][7]

7
René Charles Guilbert de Pixerécourt, *Coelina ou l'enfant du mystère*, in Paris, at Barba's bookshop, Palais-Égalité, Gallery behind the Théâtre de la République, year IX (1800).

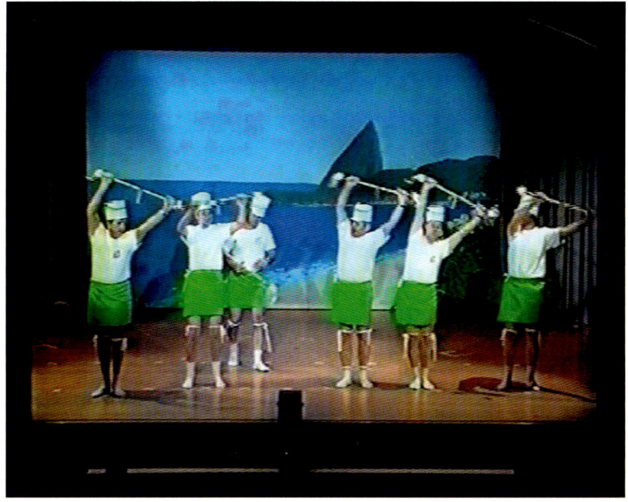
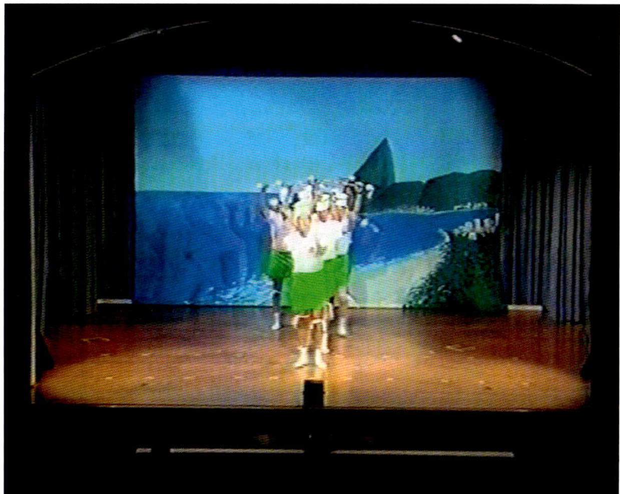

LES CHARLOTS, 2005
Video, color, silent, 3'26"
Collection Mamco, Geneva

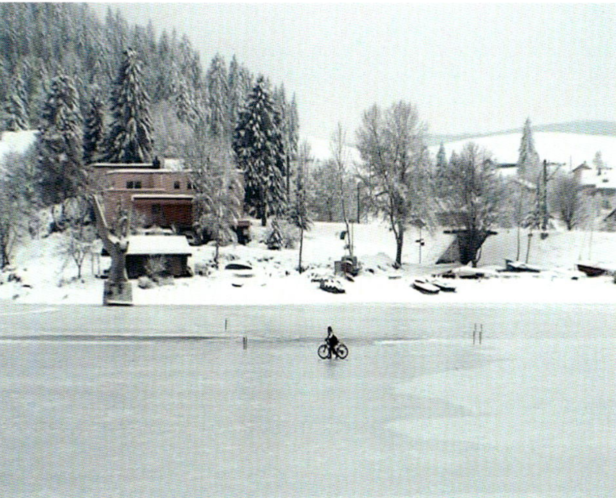

PÉGASE, 2009
Video, color, silent, 1'50"
Collection Mamco, Geneva

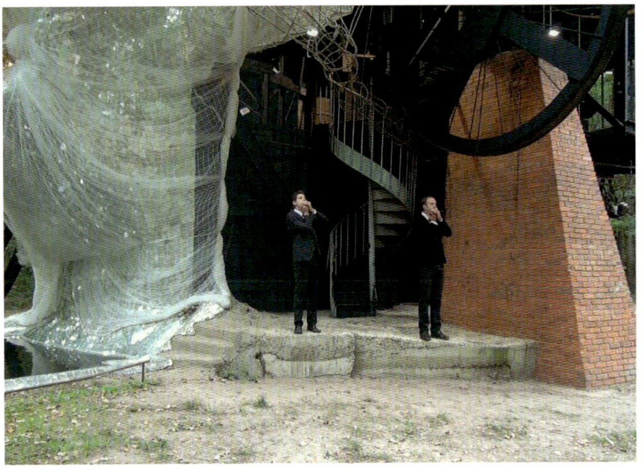

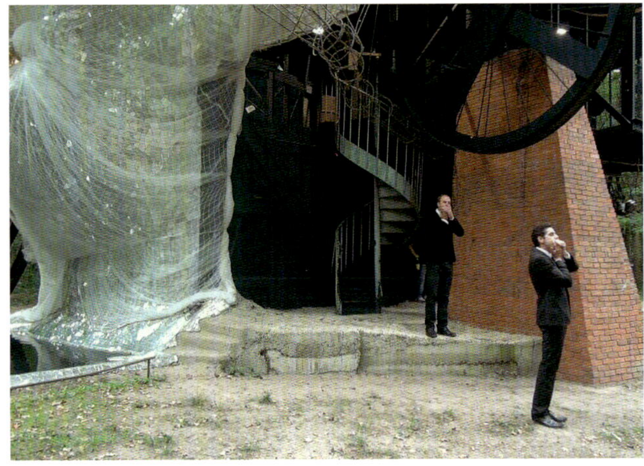

ÉTOURNEAUX, D'APRÈS L'URSONATE
DE KURT SCHWITTERS, 2013
With Jean Boucault and Johnny Rasse
Video, color, sound, 5'12"
Collection Mamco, Geneva

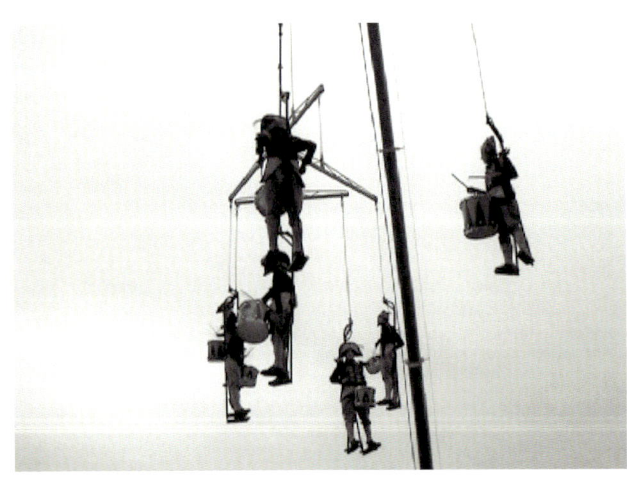

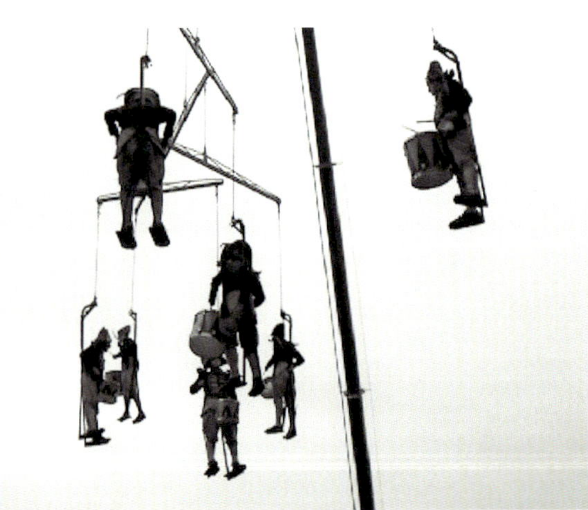

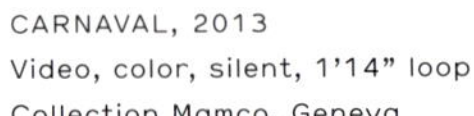

CARNAVAL, 2013
Video, color, silent, 1'14" loop
Collection Mamco, Geneva

The Ritornello
Julie Pellegrin

In 1932 Kurt Schwitters stayed at a house on a Norwegian island. Legend has it that apart from the material traces left by the artist—collages, writings, and painted plaster work—the song of the starlings in the vicinity of the house also attests to the time he spent there. These mimic birds have supposedly been relaying his sound poem, *Ursonate* (*Original Sonata*), for several generations.

Unlike this formidable living memory, a book is a defective instrument when it comes to describing an artist's work. Silent and motionless, it risks reducing a complex oeuvre solely to its visual dimension—or indeed its photogenic one. More or less perceptible movements run through Denis Savary's work, which organize it profoundly. As I write, I wonder to what extent the pages of this book will be able to describe these movements. How can the acoustic, atmospheric, mechanical, or choreographic dimensions inherent in a work or an exhibition be conveyed? How can what is invisible be made visible?

With Denis Savary, there is often nothing to see, even in his work on the image. The drawings are barely sketched, the engravings are censored, the videos frame empty spaces. The latter are sometimes "unwatchable," like *Le Must*, a still shot of the deserted dance floor of a provincial nightclub, or *Le Facteur d'orgue*, another still shot of an anonymous place—a church? a village hall?—where a couple of workmen can be heard off screen in the process of tuning an organ. In these filmed scenes, always shown in a loop, sound has primacy over the image, sometimes freeing itself from it completely. Moreover, *Le Facteur d'orgue* later became a sound piece in its own right.

In 2013 Denis Savary broadcast an interpretation of *Ursonate* in the woods surrounding *Le Cyclop* by Jean Tinguely and Niki de Saint-Phalle, with the aim of inspiring the starlings of the Forest of Fontainebleau. These birds, which are capable of varied and complex vocalizations, are well known for incorporating the sounds from their surroundings into their song—the sounds of other birds, but also of car horns, telephones, and snatches of human language. Kurt Schwitters' sound poem is interpreted here by two bird mimics, Jean Boucault and Johnny Rasse. While Kurt Schwitters respects the rhythm and melody of the traditional sonata in four movements in his composition, at the end he introduces a different musical structure, tirelessly repeating "fmsbwtözaüpggiv."[1] Perhaps it is not so much the sonata that interests Denis Savary as this ritornello or refrain—that of the bird that repeats its chorus every morning. It is embodied in figures that recur from one work to another: mimic birds (starlings, parrots) and individuals deter-mined to go on doggedly repeating the same actions (airmen, musicians), or absorbed in everyday activities. The ritornello can then be the ditty that accompanies idleness or obsession.

In *La Courtisane*, one of the artist's first videos, a hurdy-gurdy player is practicing next to a motocross track. His arm turning the wheel

1
Pronounced according to the phonetics of the German alphabet.

echoes the vehicles going round in a loop in the background. The circular motifs intersect and the noise of the engines is confused with the sound of the instrument. It is in this infernal double circle that the assignment of territory takes place, just as certain birds sing to stake out their territory. The ritornello then seems like a structural motif that basically organizes work by evoking a territorial order: like a circularity, but also like a line that turns back on itself, corrects itself, repeats itself. "In a general sense, we call a refrain any aggregate of matters of expression that draws a territory and develops into territorial motifs and landscapes (there are optical, gestural, motor, etc. refrains). In a narrow sense, we speak of a refrain when an assemblage is sonorous or 'dominated' by sound."[2]

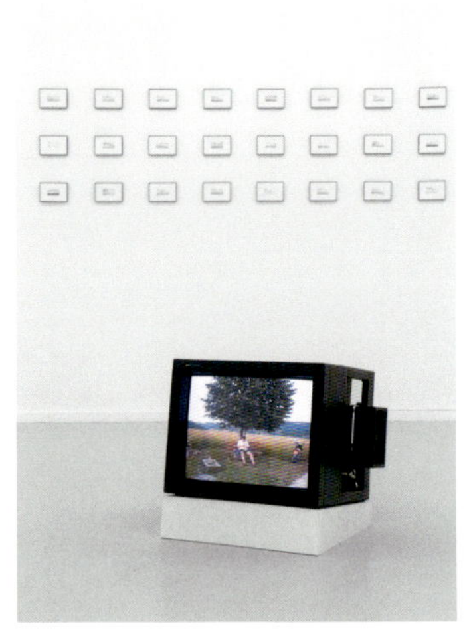

On the wall: Morio, LA LONGUE ROUTE, 2008–2010, pencil lead on paper, 6.2 × 3.8 cm each
Foreground: BRÎT, 2004, video, color, sound, 6'09"
Exhibition view, *Carrousel*, La Ferme du Buisson, Noisiel, 2010
Photo: Aurélien Mole

In Denis Savary's work, the ritornello or refrain is often based on sound, but it can also be gestural, visual, spatial, and temporal. Drawn into a circular mechanism, both the works and the people go round and round, powered by engines—tires or plants being transformed into roundabouts—or by their own dynamics—fountains and other closed circuits. In his exhibition at the Centre d'art contemporain de La Ferme du Buisson, actually entitled *Carrousel*, the circle of grimacing busts responded to that of the *Alma* dolls, suspended from the framework, a distant reminder of Henri Matisse's *La Danse*.

The circular movement brings into play centrifugal forces that are able to get the better of weight. They grip central vacuums round which events start moving and tend to rise. As a corollary there is the omnipresence of breath: that of the birds, of the musician warming up on the trumpet, of the burners on hot air balloons, of the wind required for the lift-off of Captain Ferber's machines.

In the films and sculptures, the emptiness of the image directs attention to the sounds off-screen. For Denis Savary it is sound that crystallizes the cinematographic dimension. For example, the kinetoscope wheelbarrows devised with Jean-Marc Chapoulie to project films were transformed a few exhibitions later into kinetophones: three black holes broadcasting *Le Régiment de Sambre et Meuse*, which Thomas Edison played to his projectionists to help them keep the correct rhythm for running the images.

Little by little the bird builds its nest ... In concentric circles, this logic of the ritornello spreads from the work to the whole exhibition. Extended, the soundtrack plays a full part in its dramaturgy. The space was entirely bathed in the sound of breath at the the Centre d'art contemporain de La Ferme du Buisson, of birdsong in Bienne, and of cracklings at the Villa Bernasconi. At Les Arques, the whole village, "so motionless that it looks like a set," was animated by the sounds of horse riding being played on street corners.

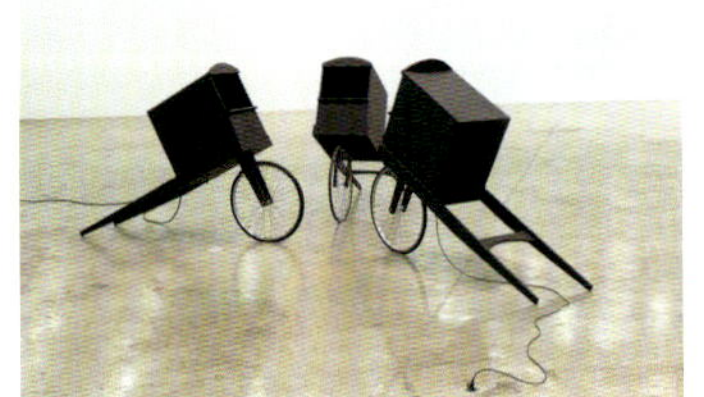

SAMBRE & MEUSE, 2010
Wood, black paint, bicycle wheels, sound system, 150 × 50.5 × 177 cm each

Thus the ritornello is a way of giving the exhibition rhythm and setting its duration. It draws temporal territories that coexist, and that are sometimes superimposed. The past regularly resurfaces in the present, in a practice haunted by historical figures (Captain Ferber, Pierre Klossowski, Camille Corot), or anonymous presences that rise up like ghosts. *Victorine*, the dance solo written with Delphine Lorenzo, is conveyed in the exhibition by a black table that creaks under the steps

2
Gilles Deleuze and Félix Guattari, *A Thousand Plateaus. Capitalism and Schizophrenia* (1980), Bloomsbury Academic, London 2013, p. 321.

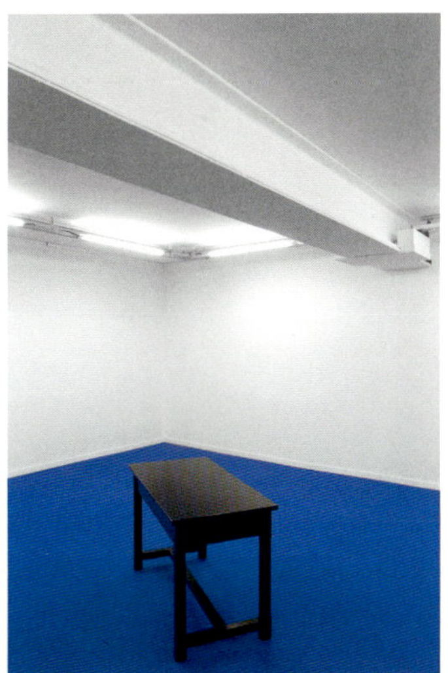

VICTORINE (LA TABLE), 2010
In collaboration with Delphine Lorenzo
Painted wood, sound
Exhibition view, *Carrousel*, La Ferme du Buisson, Noisiel, 2010
Photo: Aurélien Mole

of an invisible dancer. Alma, the doll commissioned by Oscar Kokoschka to replace his mistress who had run away, is brought back to life by a dressmaker, in several, always slightly different, versions.

Invited to the Crac Languedoc-Roussillon for a project in collaboration with artist Philippe Ramette, Denis Savary chose to work only on the exhibition's soundtrack. Lasting 80 minutes, it creates a circular movement that "switches on" the concrete architecture. The work is a way of implying the length of the visit: 80 minutes to see the whole thing, like around the world in 80 days. But a single track moves from room to room. The viewer is always late or early, never where they should be. This results in a form of suspense, with the soundtrack, devised as if for a film noir, dramatizing the works exhibited by Philippe Ramette.

At the Kunsthalle in Bern, the exhibition seemed to be completely designed as a piece of music composed of several ritornellos at different tempos. The works themselves started to stammer, following the example of *Le Must*, which reappears several times in different formats. An eternal return accompanied in the last room by ... the twitter of starlings.

The ritornello sets in motion the activity of the bodies and works, all of them transformed into obsessive presences. In parallel, its rhythmic pattern makes it possible to organize the exhibition as a space of exchange and movement. It establishes structures of actions and repetitions that facilitate the appropriation of the physical and symbolic space by the viewer. The refrain or circle produces a space-time learning process, a ritualization of inhabitation. The artist often thinks of his exhibition spaces as spaces to be lived in, and likes to quote Simonide de Céos, a Greek poet at the origin of a mnemonic method—the "loci" mnemonic method—based on remembering places. Perhaps the ritornello corresponds first and foremost to an art of memory. Thus the exhibition is seen, heard, experienced, and already committed to memory, all in one go. And visitors, like Kurt Schwitters' starlings, become the finest living memory of it.

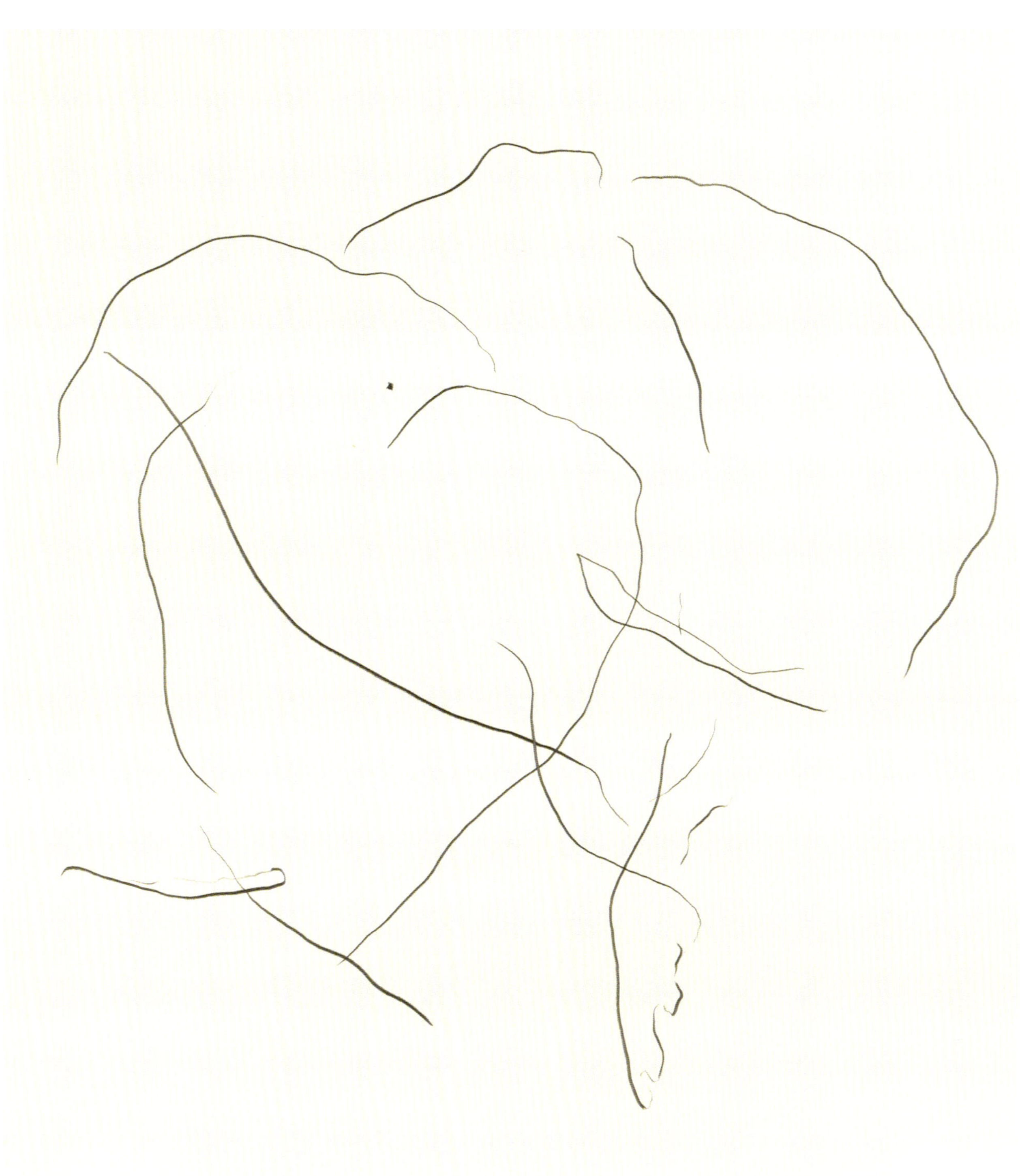

UNTITLED, 2013

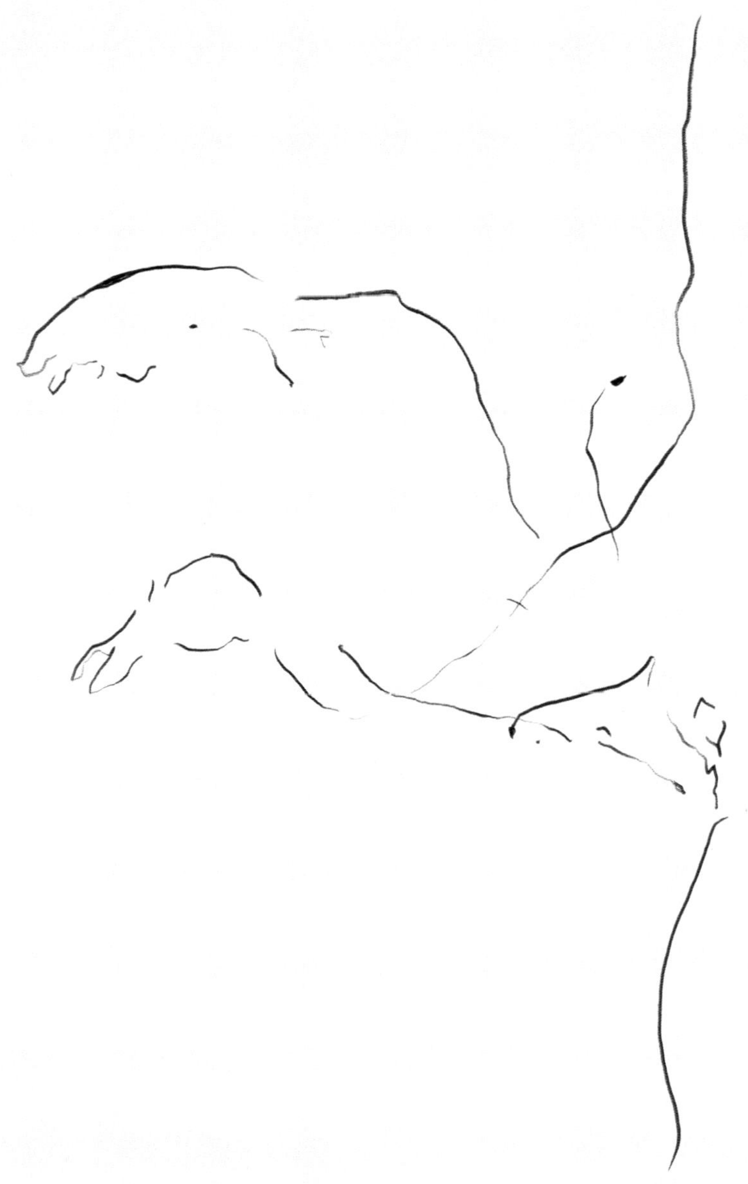

UNTITLED, 2012

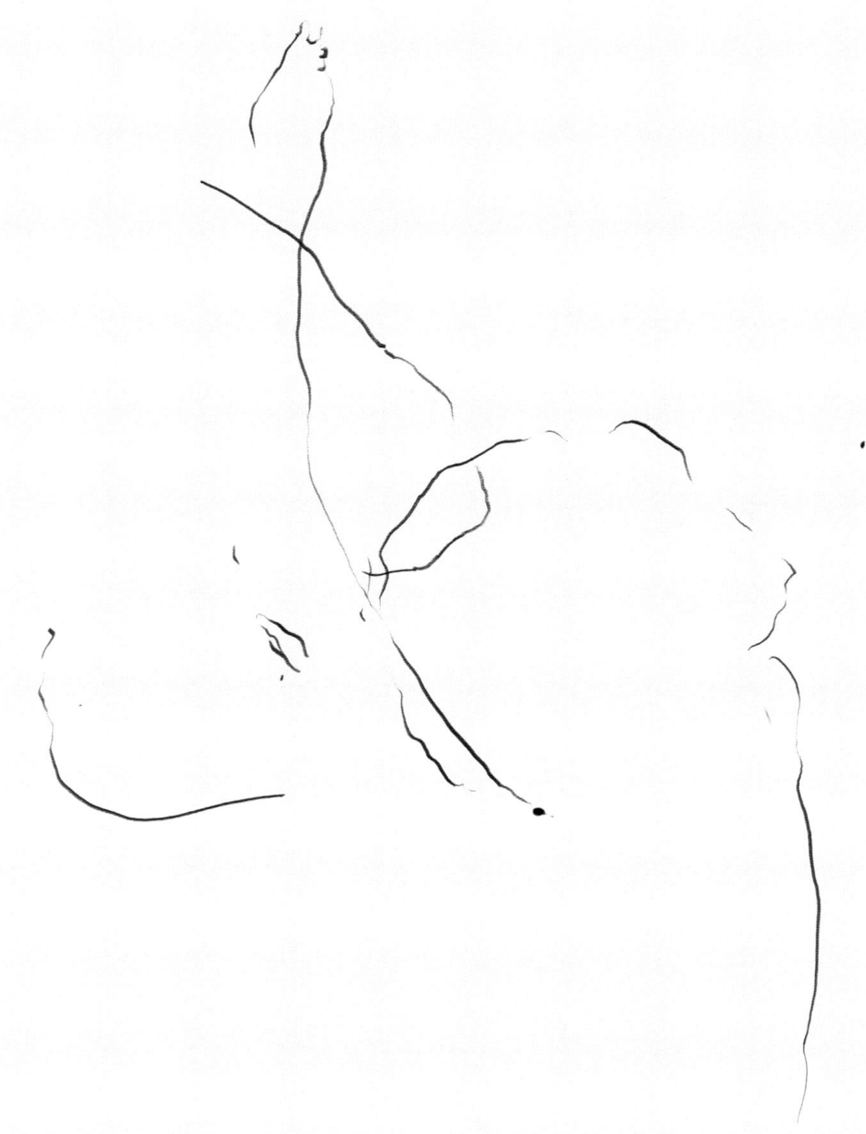

UNTITLED, 2013

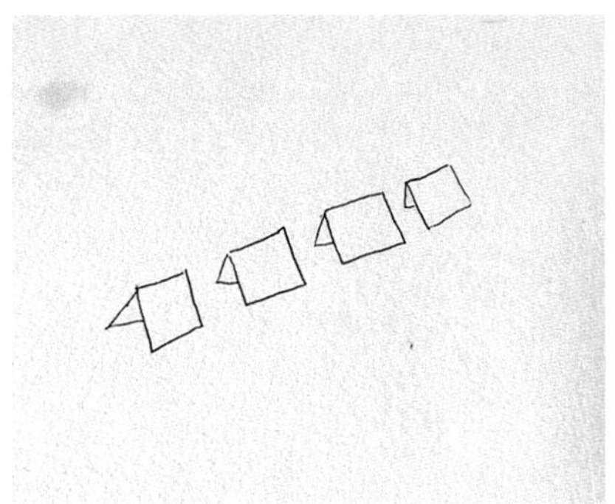
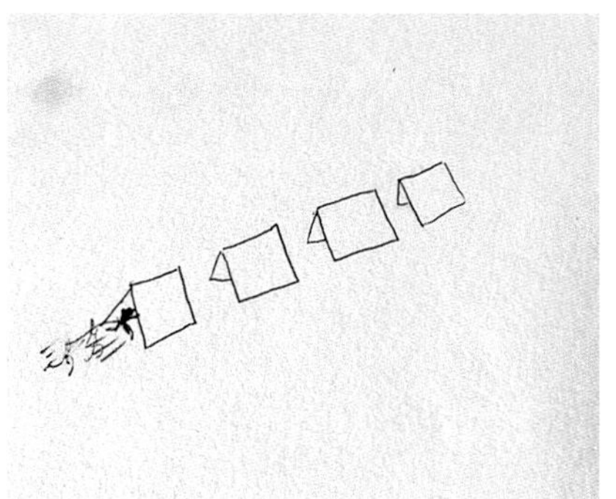
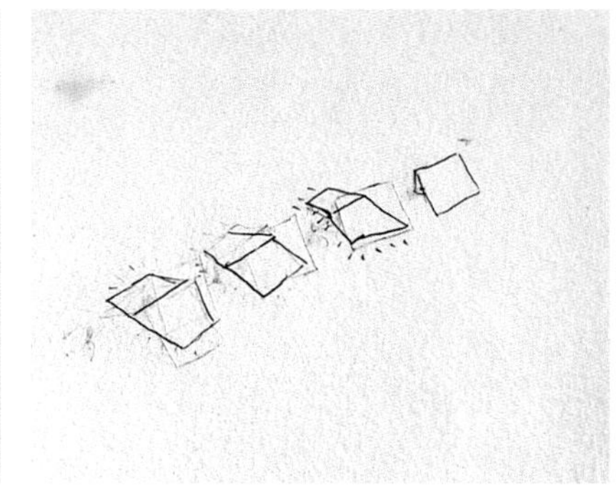
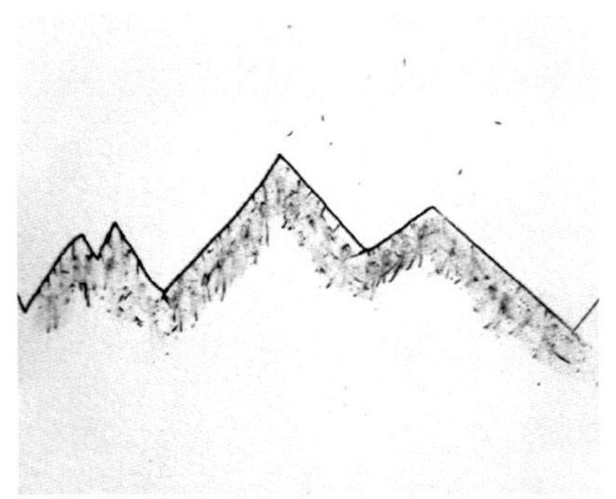
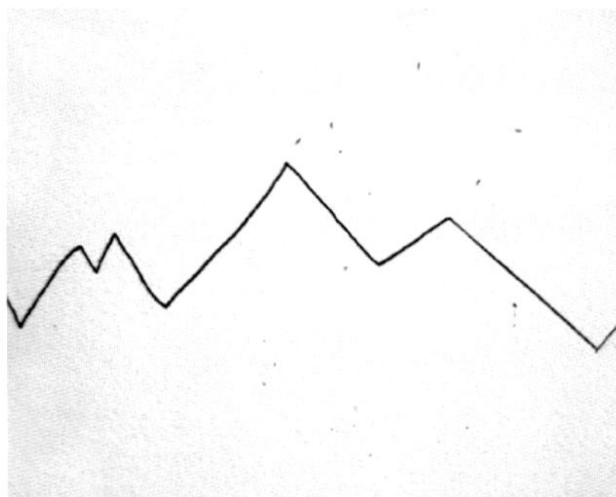
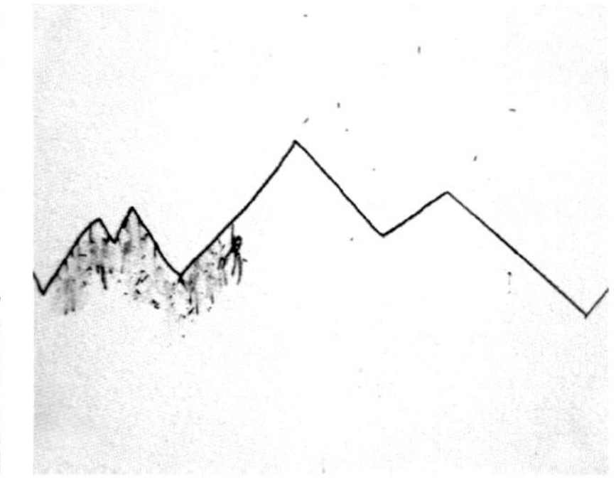
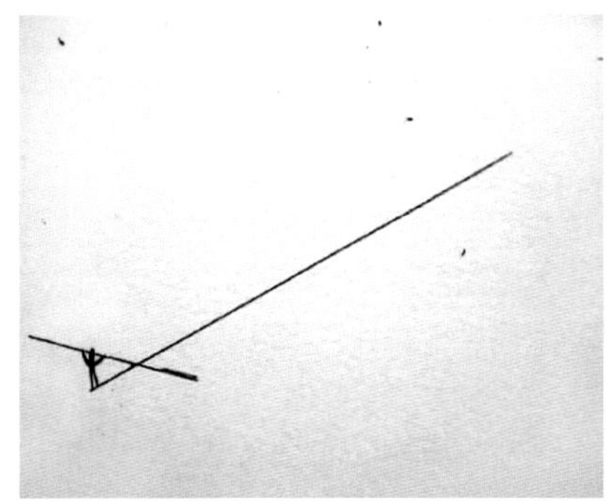
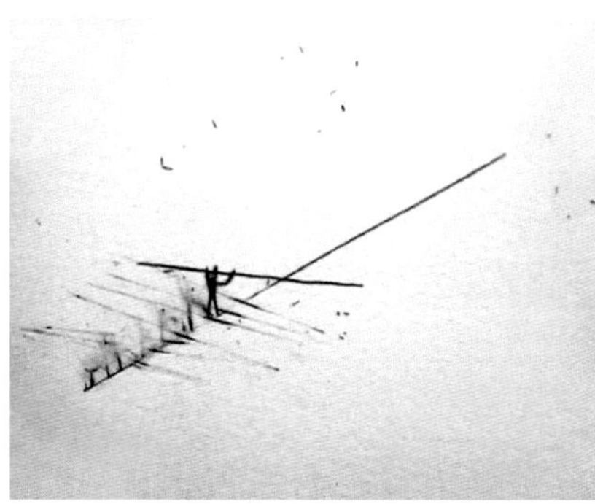
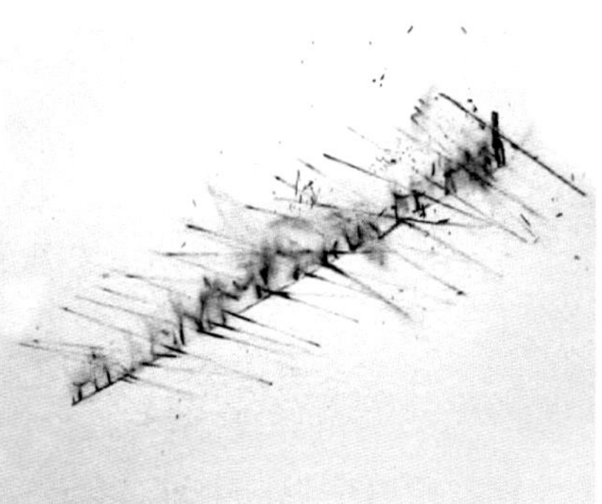

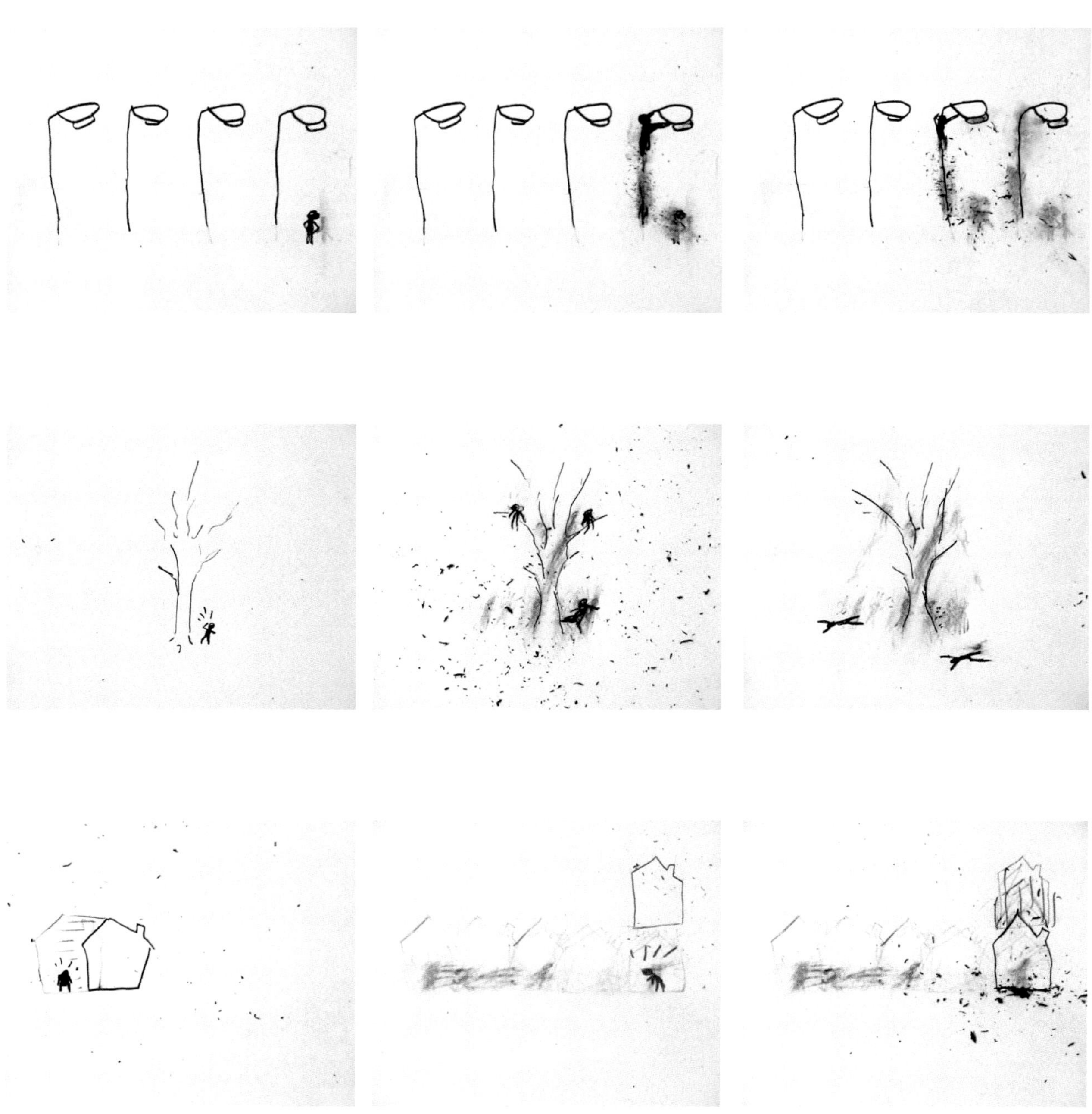

UNTITLED, 2008

UNTITLED, 2008

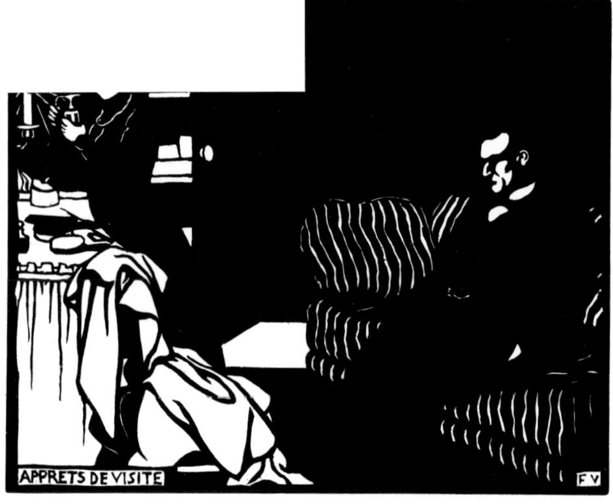
APPRETS DE VISITE
FV

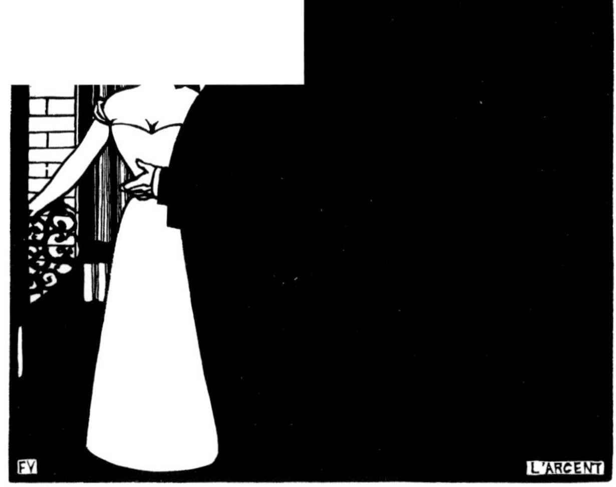
FV
L'ARGENT

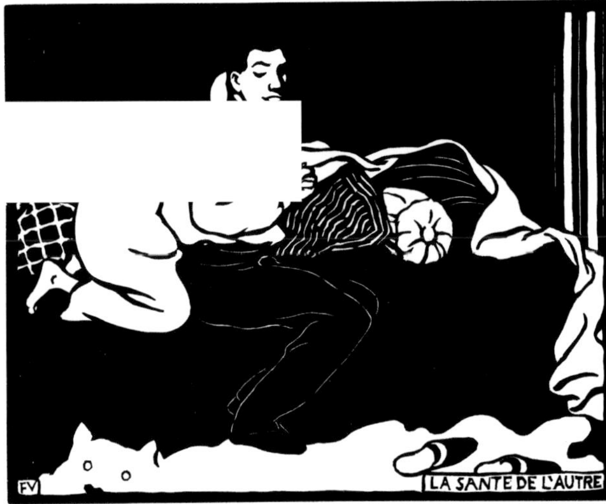
FV
LA SANTE DE L'AUTRE

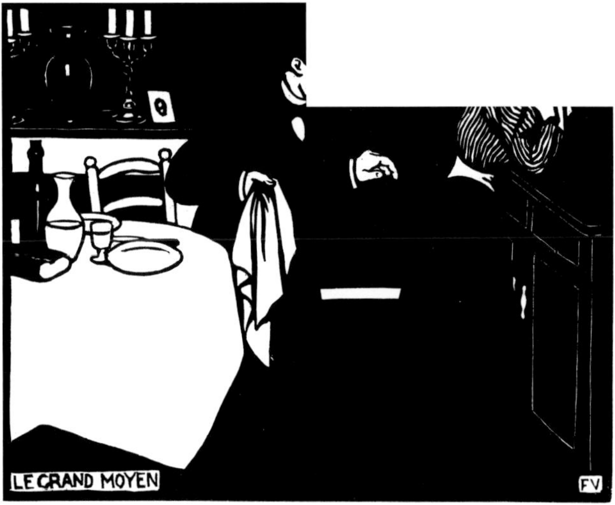
LE GRAND MOYEN
FV

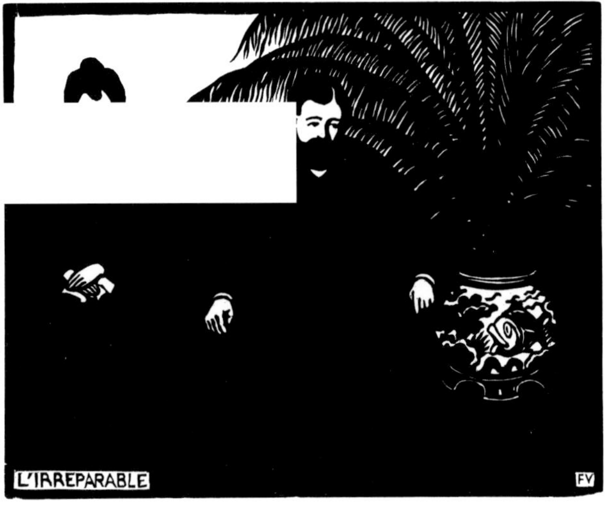
L'IRREPARABLE
FV

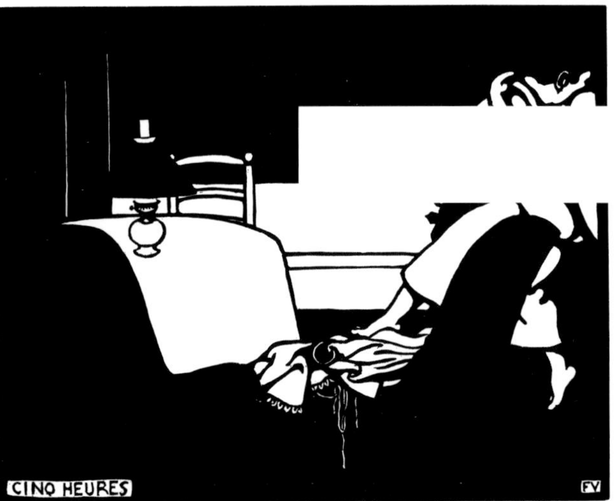
CINQ HEURES
FV

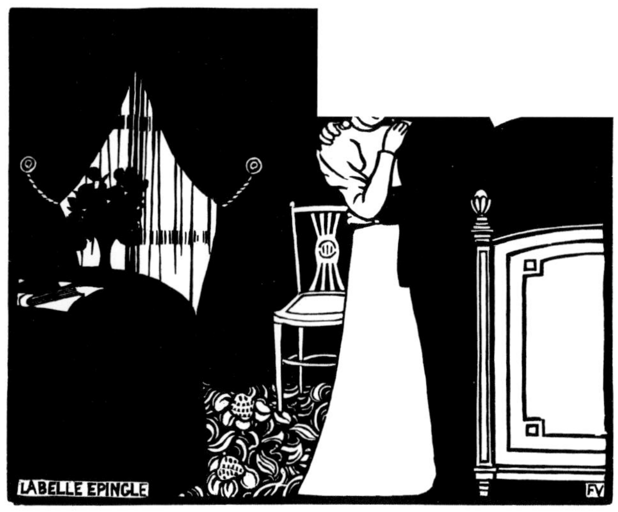
LA BELLE EPINGLE
FV

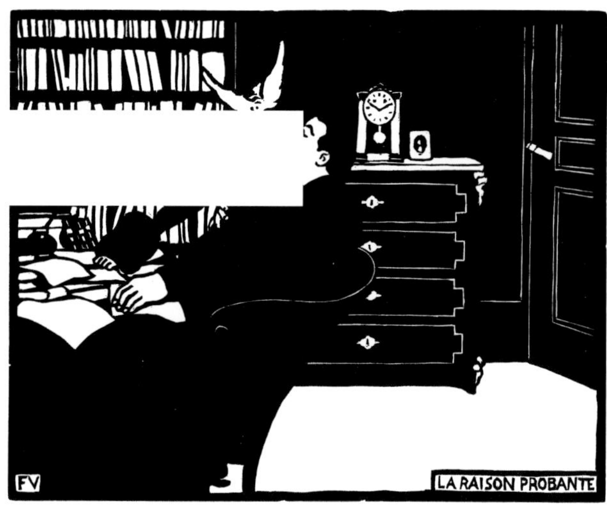
FV
LA RAISON PROBANTE

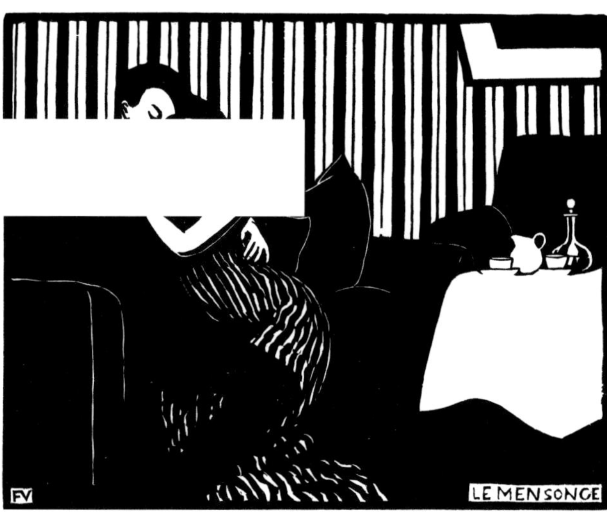
FV
LE MENSONGE

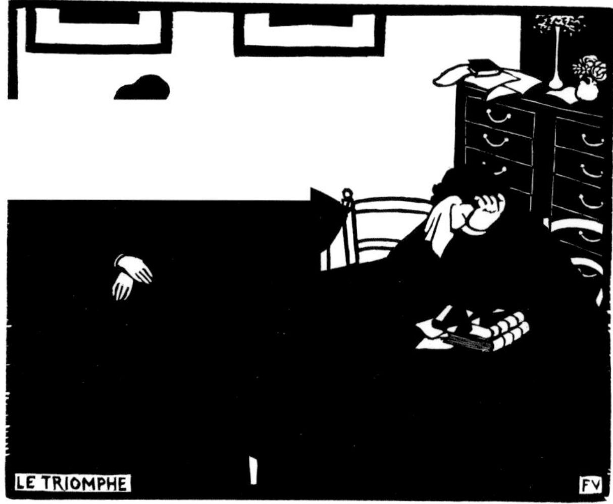
LE TRIOMPHE
FV

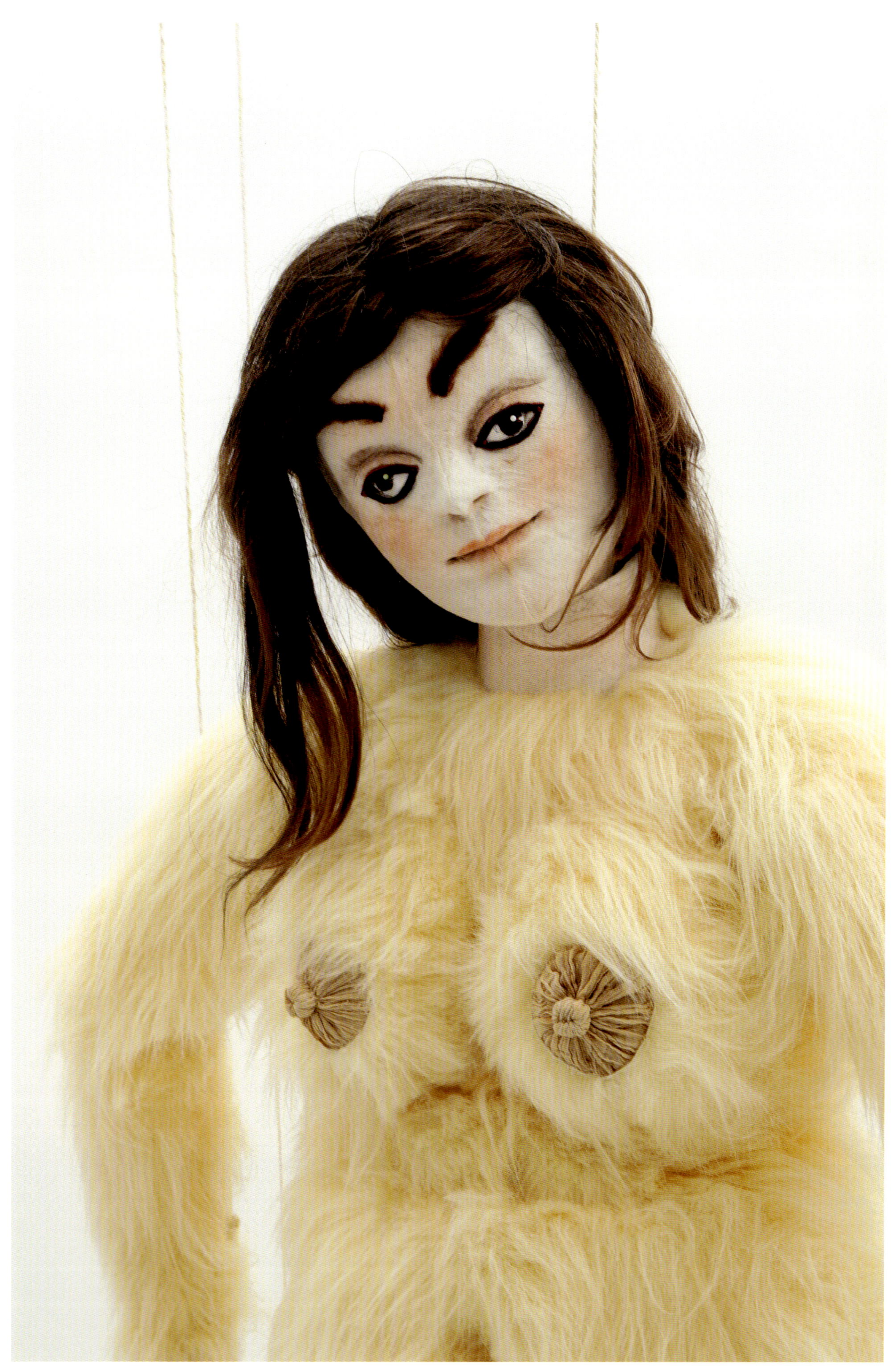

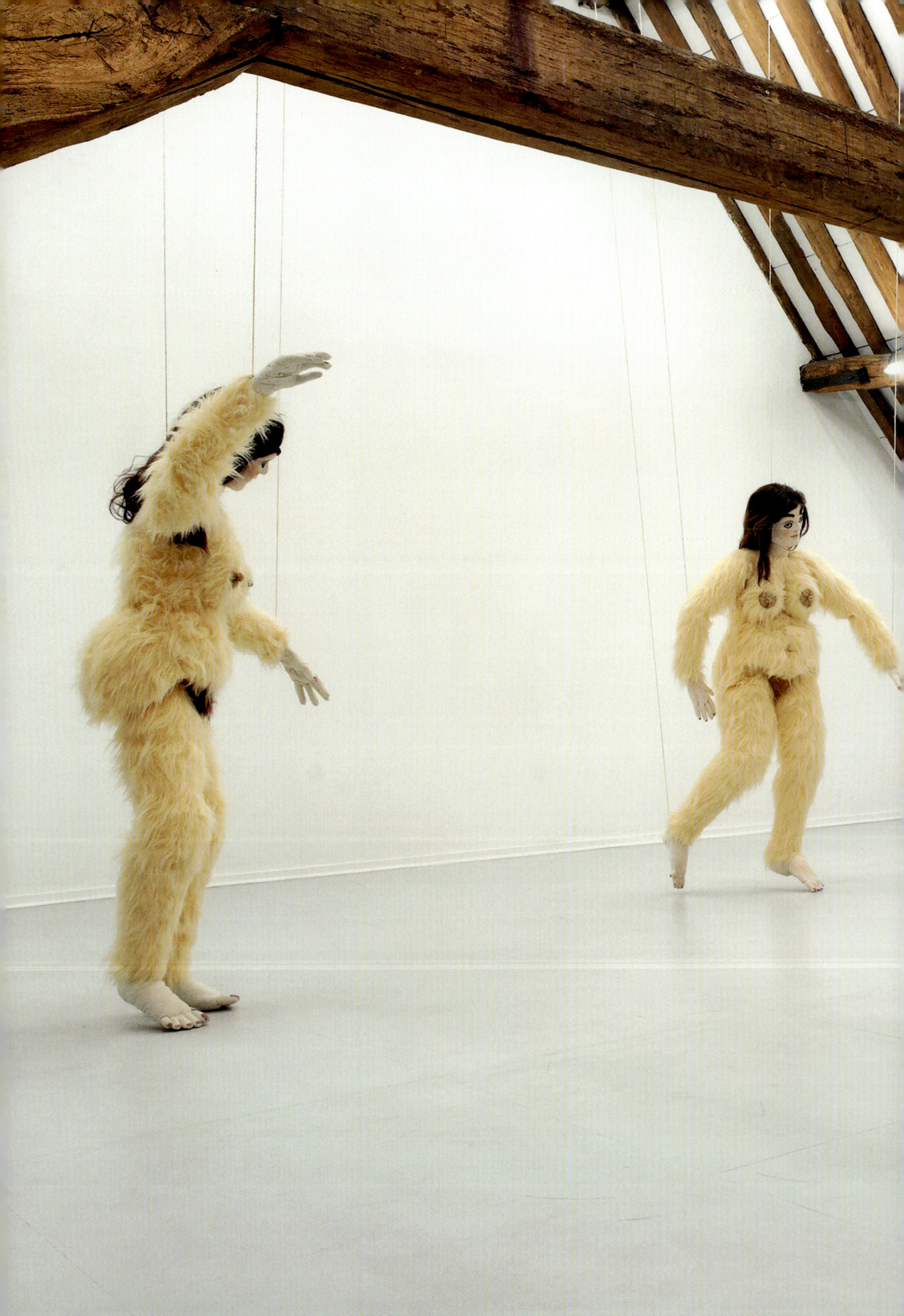

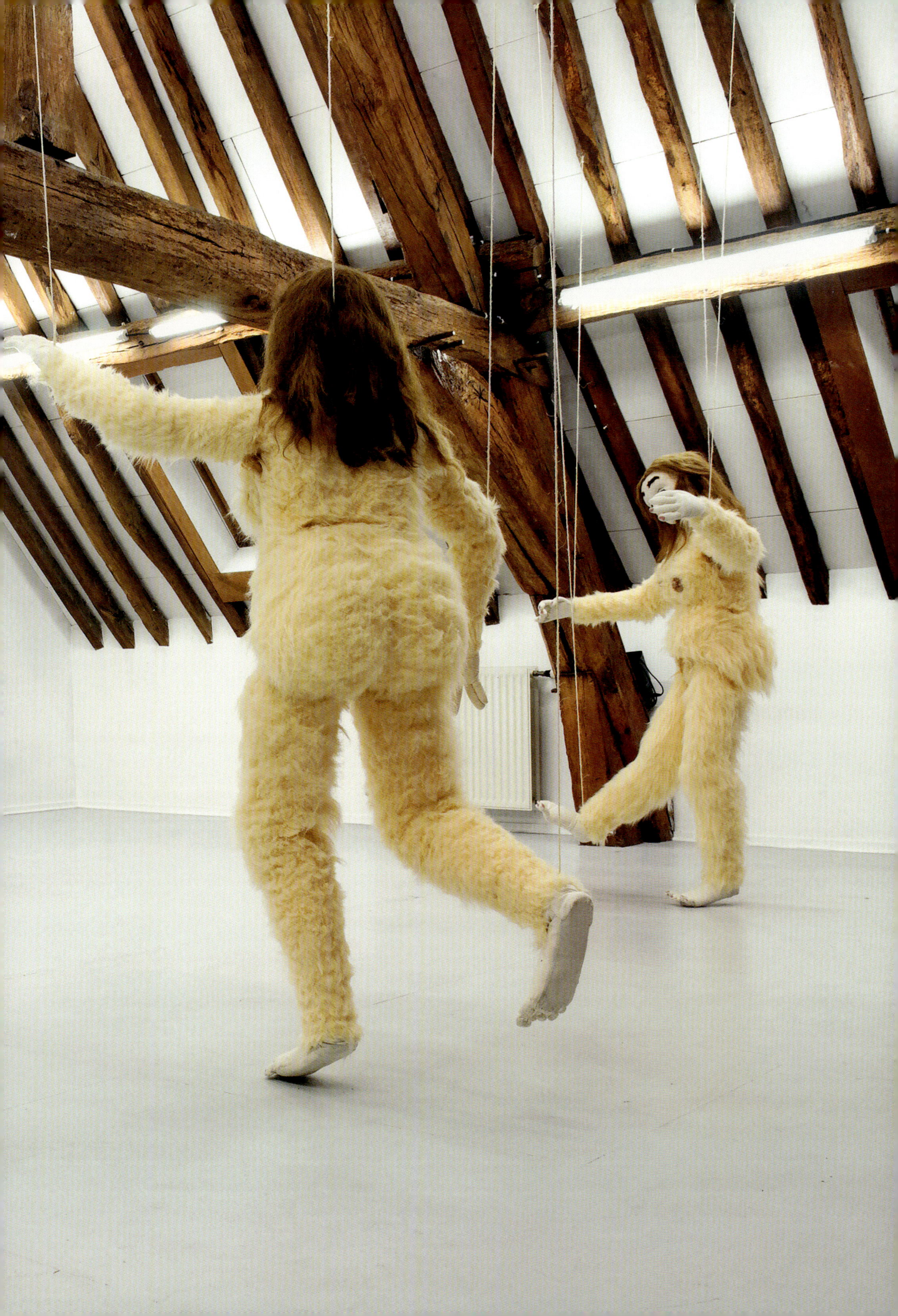

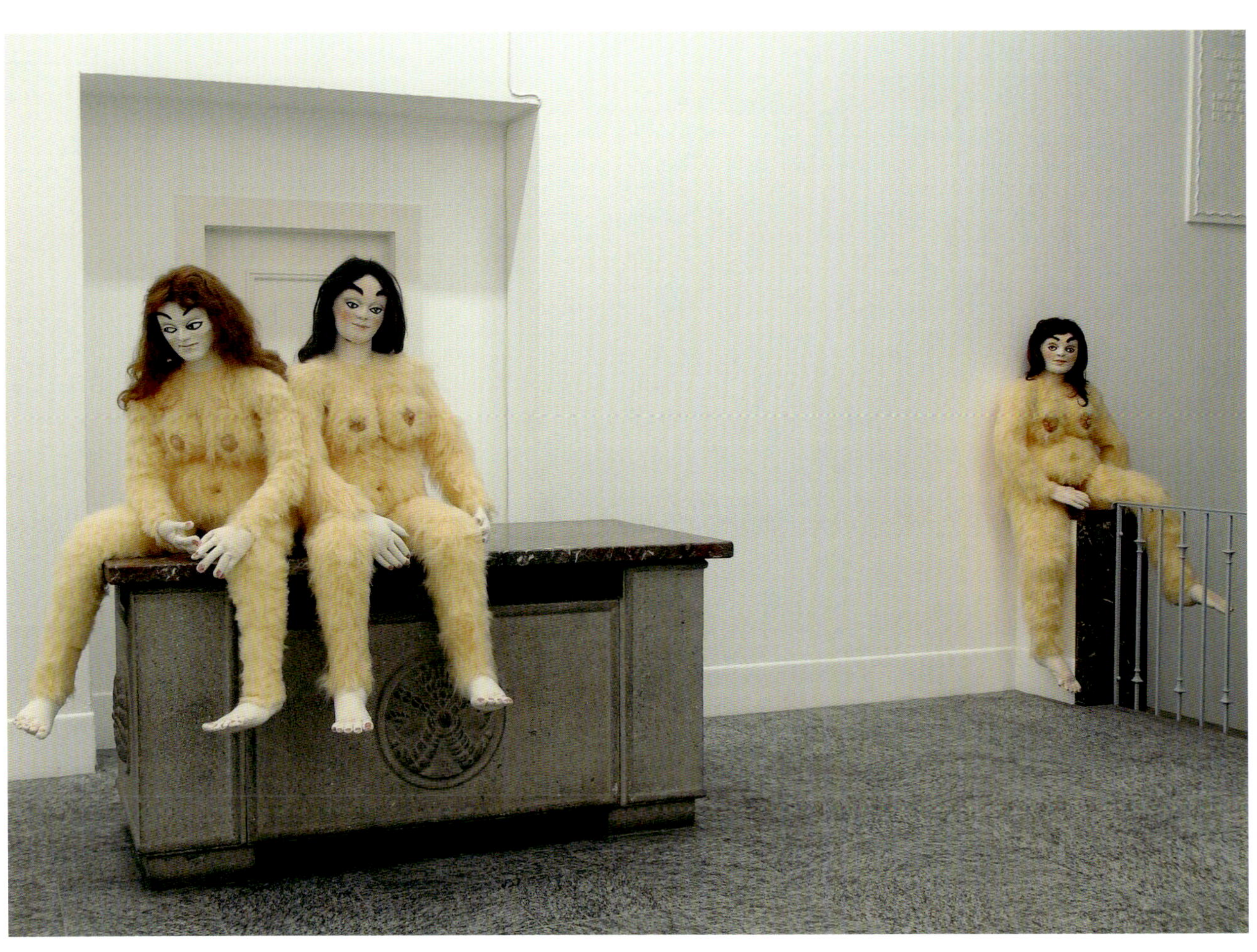

← ALMA, D'APRÈS OSKAR KOKOSCHKA, 2007, exhibition view, *Carrousel*, La Ferme du Buisson, Noisiel, 2010

ALMA, D'APRÈS OSKAR KOKOSCHKA, 2007, exhibition views, *Baltiques*, Kunsthalle Bern, 2012

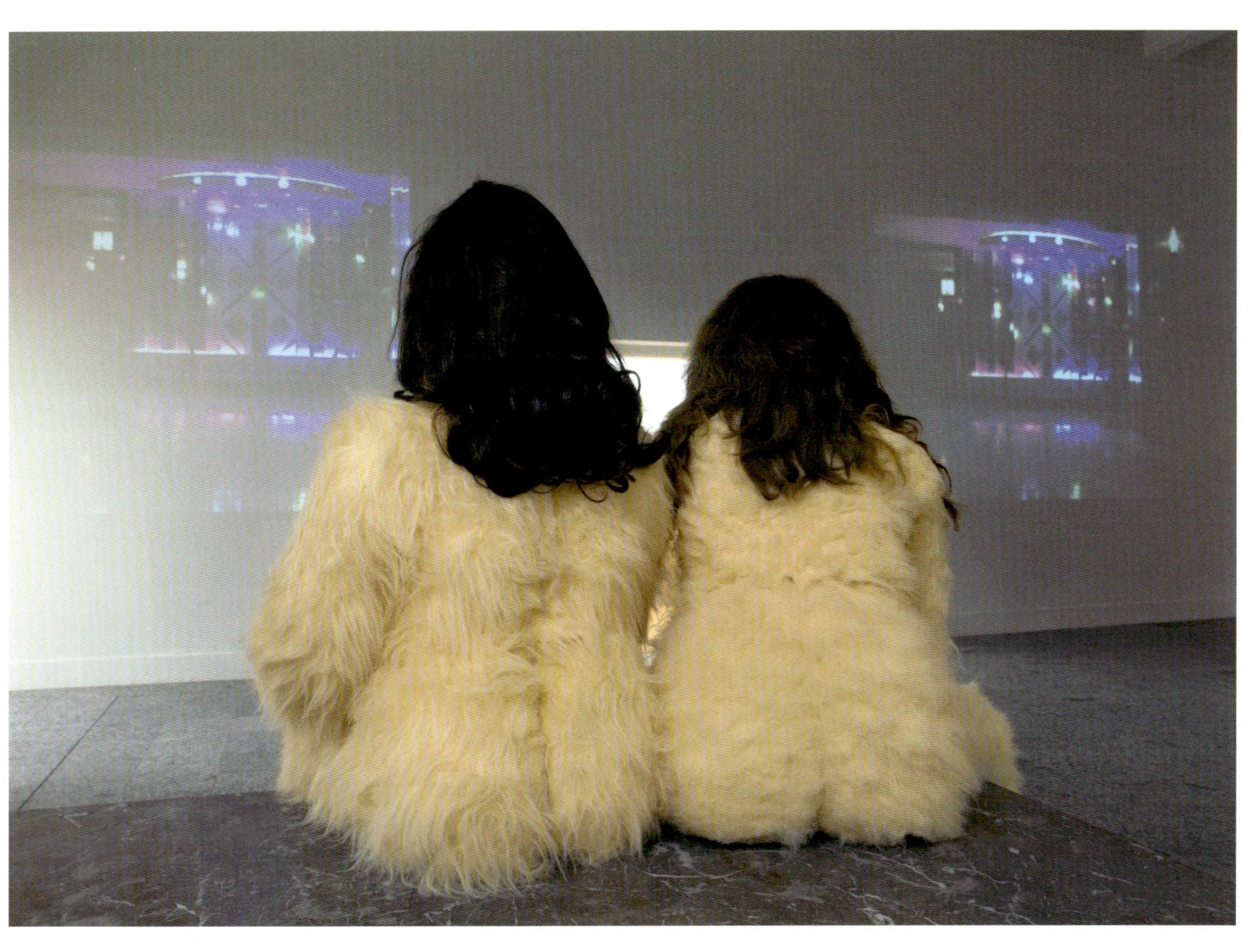

Exhibition view, *Carrousel*, La Ferme du Buisson, Noisiel, 2010
With LES GRIMACES D'APRÈS LUC ANDRIÉ, 2008, and LE MUST, 2004

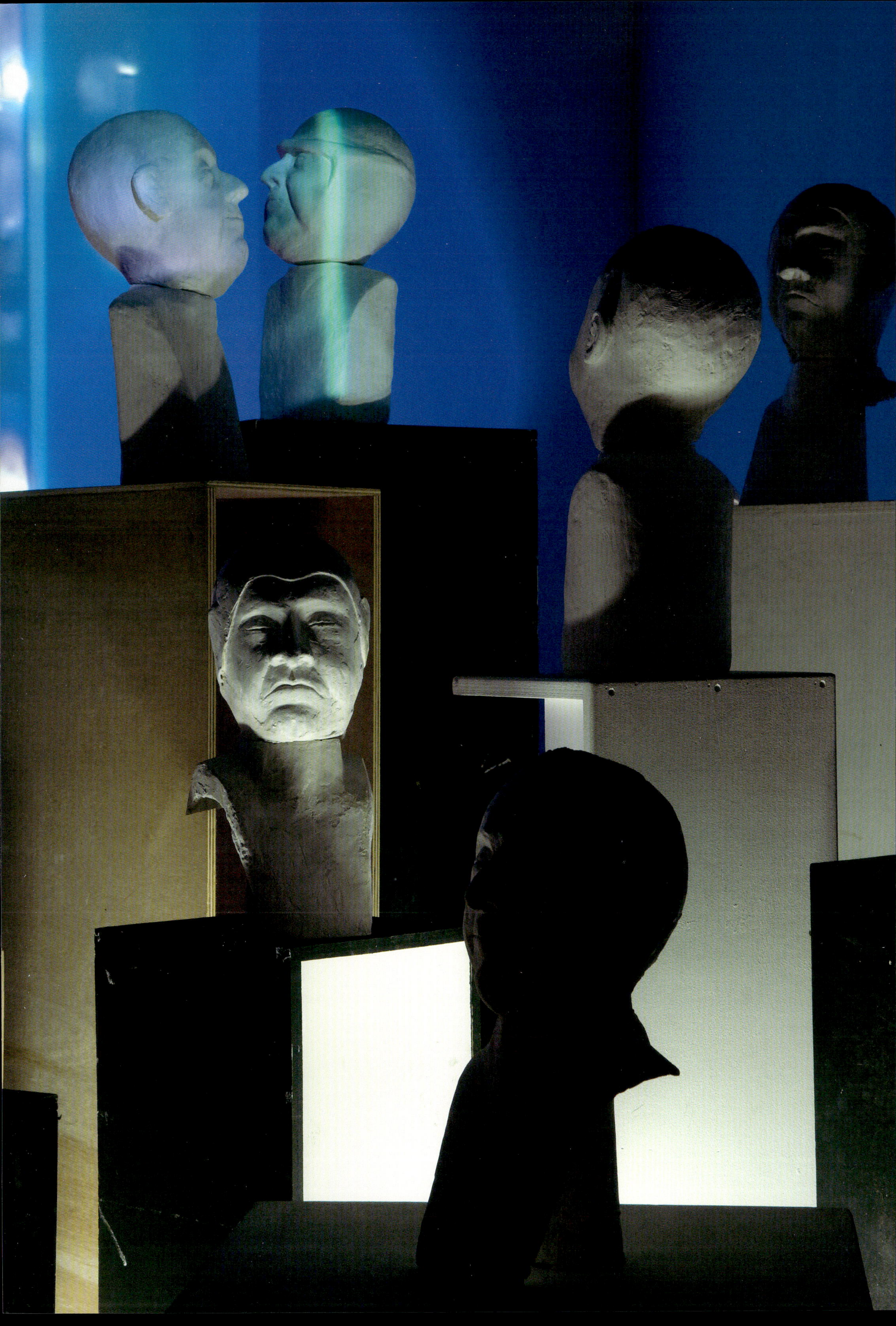

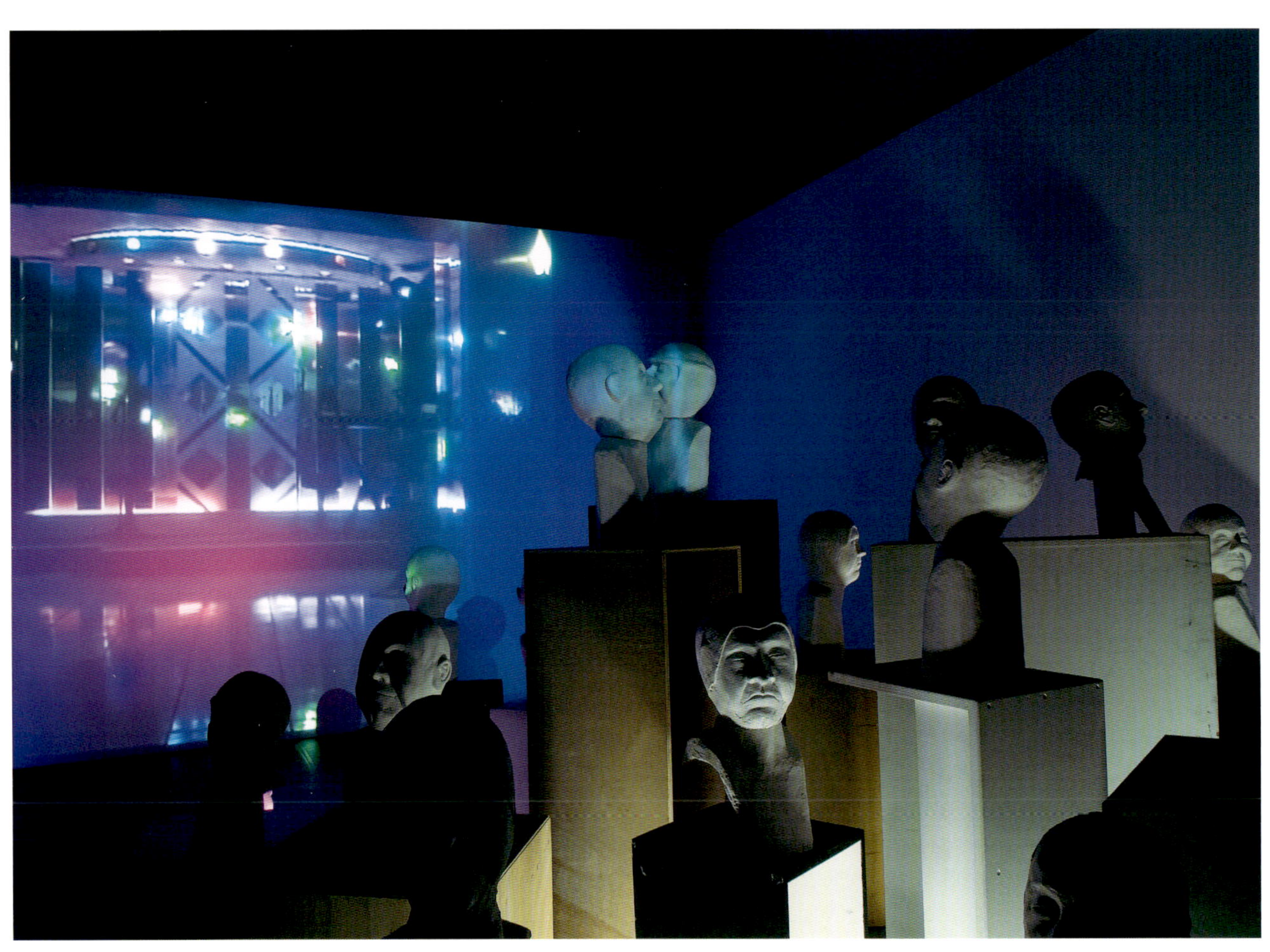

Exhibition view, *Carrousel*, La Ferme du Buisson, Noisiel, 2010

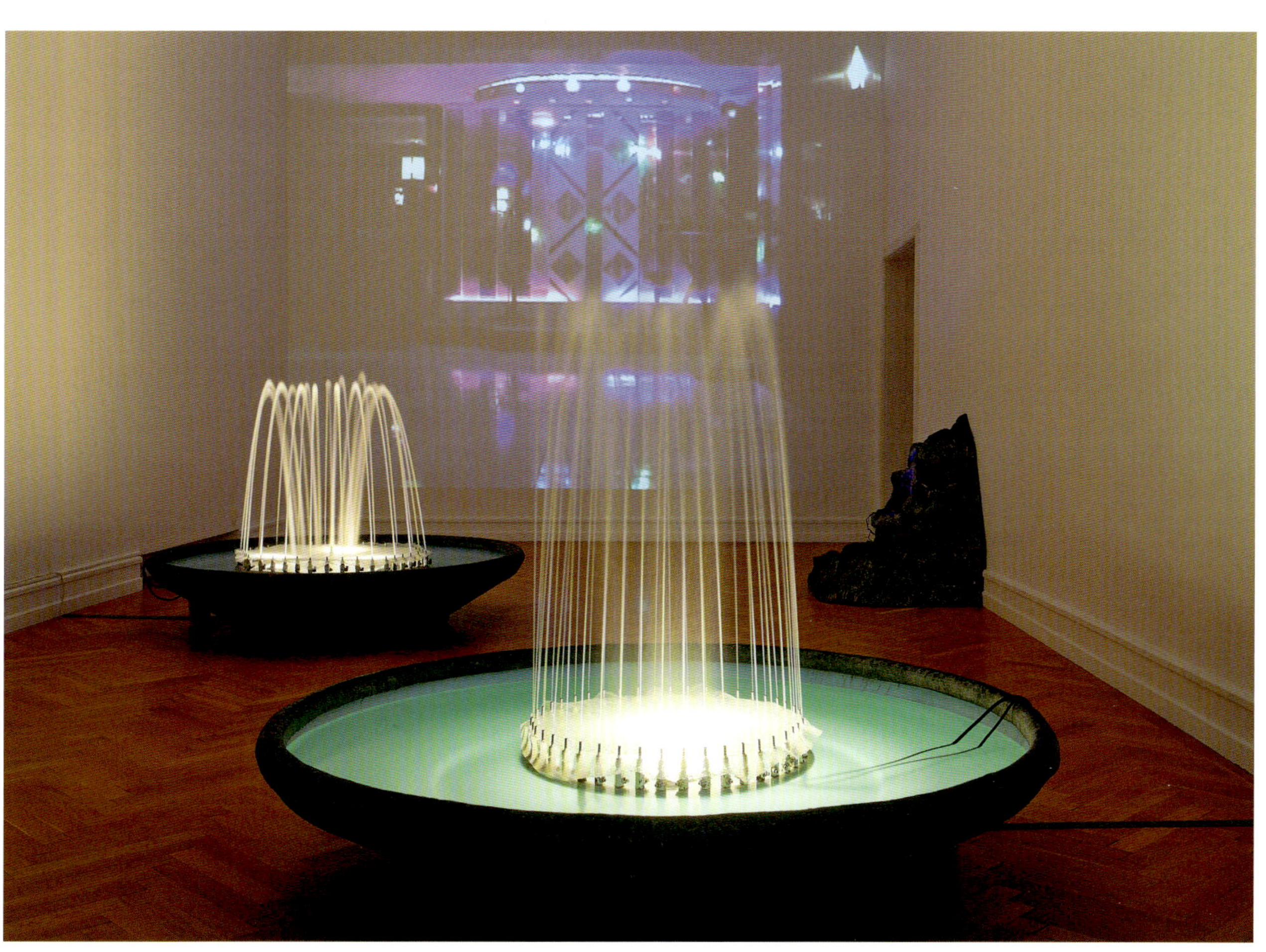

Exhibition view, *Baltiques*, Kunsthalle Bern, 2012

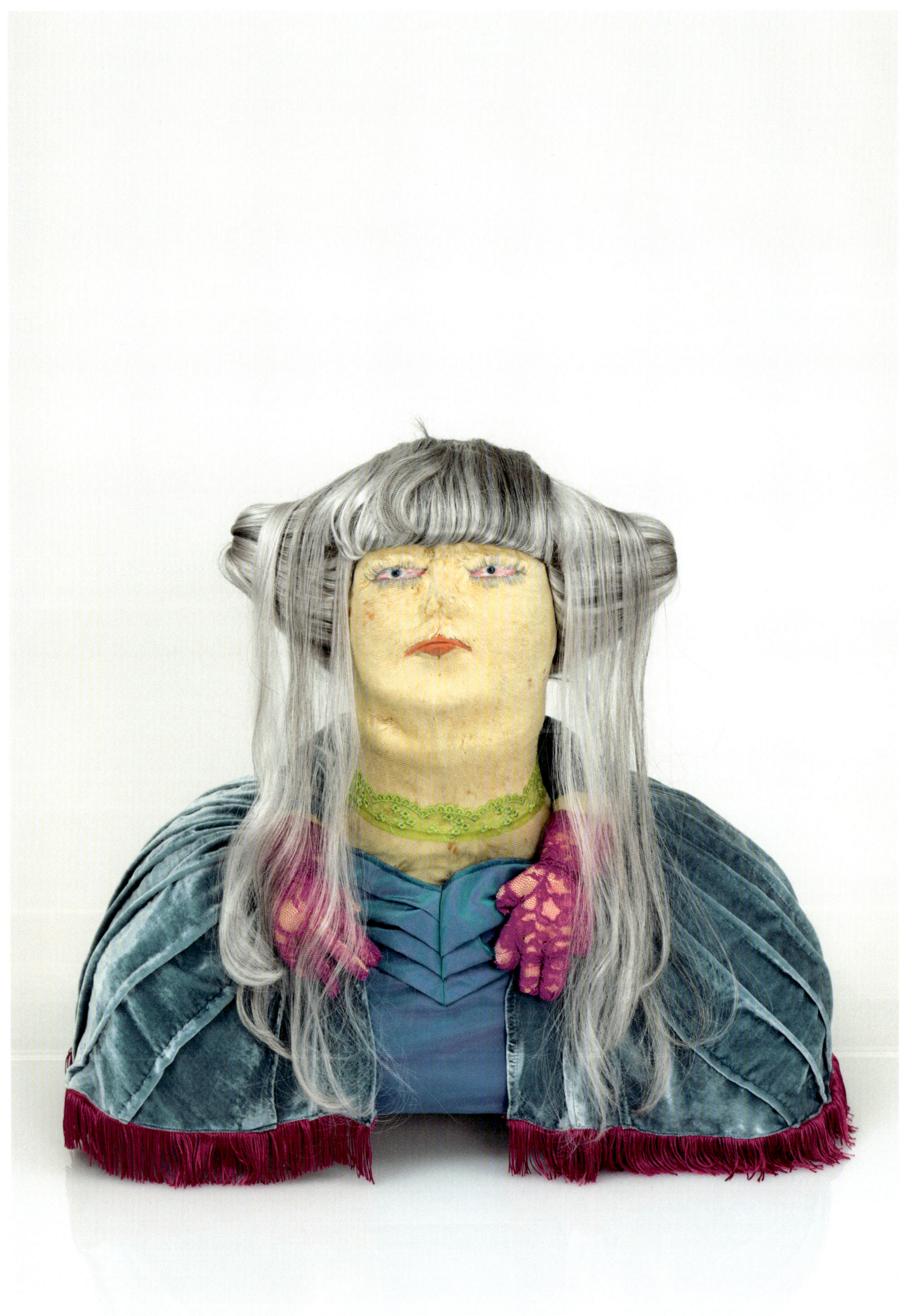

MARIE-LOUISE, 2013

List of Works

[Cover] *Intimités, d'après Félix Vallotton: L'Irréparable*, 2007 (detail)
Silkscreen, 30 × 36 cm

[p. 3, 4–5] *Maison de poupée*, 2008
Exterior view and interior details; wood, paint, plastic, 85 × 90 × 56.5 cm
Collection Nicole Timonier
Photos: Annik Wetter

[p. 7] *Métier II*, 2010
Wood, straps, black paint, height of pole: 180 cm, structure: 107.5 × 48.5 × 44.5 cm
Photo: Annik Wetter

[p. 8] *Métier III*, 2010
Wood, straps, black paint, 101 × 60 × 49 cm
Exhibition view, *Carrousel*, La Ferme du Buisson, Noisiel, 2010
Photo: Aurélien Mole

[p. 9] Left: *Métier IV (La Girafe)*, 2010
Wood, black paint, 160.5 × 65 × 25 cm
Exhibition view, *Carrousel*, La Ferme du Buisson, Noisiel, 2010
Photo: Aurélien Mole
Right: *Métier V (Le Porteur d'eau)*, 2011
Wood, fabric, black paint, height of pole: 180 cm, structure: 108 × 55 × 50 cm
Collection Musée cantonal des Beaux-Arts, Lausanne
Photo: Annik Wetter

[p. 10] *Cheminée*, 2011
Wood, strap, black paint, 22 × 120 × 60 cm (closed), 102.5 × 120 × 60 cm (open)

[p. 11] *Cuisine*, 2012
Wood, foam, silver fabric, 72 × 160 × 60 cm
Production: Juliette Roduit & Réanne Clot
Photo: Annik Wetter

[p. 12–13] *Georgia*, 2011
Wood, glass, fabric, 190 × 30 × 40 cm
p. 12: Exhibition view, *Baltiques*, Kunsthalle Bern, 2012
Collection Stiftung Kunsthalle Bern
Photo: Annik Wetter

[p. 14–15] *Maldoror*, 2012
Wood, pigment, 250 × 225 × 225 cm each
Exhibition view, *Baltiques*, Kunsthalle Bern, 2012
Photo: Annik Wetter

[p. 17] *Alexandre*, 2012
Metal, paint, 170 × 110 × 90 cm
Exhibition view, *Baltiques*, Kunsthalle Bern, 2012
Production: Evelyne Villaime
Collection Stiftung Kunsthalle Bern
Photo: Annik Wetter

[p. 18–19] *Les Mannequins de Corot: Moules*, 2013
Wood, rubber, dimensions variable
Exhibition view, *Les Mannequins de Corot*, Musée d'Art et d'Histoire, Geneva, 2013
Production: Bernard Bordet
Photo: Annik Wetter

[p. 20–21] *Augustes*, 2013
7 sculptures, papier-mâché, latex, glass marble, pigment, silk, 43 × 57 × 45 cm each
Exhibition view, *Denis Savary*, Xippas Art Contemporain, Geneva, 2013
Production: Evelyne Villaime
Photo: Annik Wetter

[p. 22] *Ostende, d'après James Ensor*, 2011
Wood and fabric bench, elastomer mask; bench: 156 × 66 × 75 cm, mask: 22 × 64 × 19 cm
Production: Evelyne Villaime
Collection Stiftung Kunsthalle Bern

[p. 41] *Untitled*, 2013
Pencil lead on paper, 50 × 50 cm

[p. 42] *Untitled*, 2012
Pencil lead on paper, 50 × 50 cm
Collection Musée cantonal des Beaux-Arts, Lausanne

[p. 43] *Untitled*, 2012
Pencil lead on paper, 50 × 50 cm
Collection Musée cantonal des Beaux-Arts, Lausanne

[p. 44] *Le Bourdon*, 2004–2007
Animation, 15'30"

[p. 45] *Bobigny*, 2010
Animation, 17'51"

[p. 46] *Untitled*, 2008
Pencil lead on paper, 29.7 × 21 cm

[p. 47] *Untitled*, 2008
Pencil lead on paper, 29.7 × 21 cm

[p. 48–49] *Intimités, d'après Félix Vallotton*, 2007
Series of 10 silkscreens, 30 × 36 cm each
Edition of 25 + 5 copies produced by Musée Jenisch Vevey, Vevey
Collections Banque Nationale de France, Paris; Fonds National d'Art Contemporain, Paris; Artothèque départementale du Lot, Cahors

[p. 51] *Alma, d'après Oskar Kokoschka*, 2007
Mixed media, height: 168 cm, measurements: 98-78-98, edition of 3
Exhibition view, *Carrousel*, La Ferme du Buisson, Noisiel, 2010
Production: Fanny J. Terribilini
Photo: Aurélien Mole

[p. 52–53] *Alma, d'après Oskar Kokoschka*, 2007
Exhibition view, *Carrousel*, La Ferme du Buisson, Noisiel, 2010
Collections Fonds National d'Art contemporain, Paris; Mamco, Geneva; FRAC des Pays de la Loire, Carquefou; Musée Jenisch Vevey, Vevey
Photo: Aurélien Mole

[p. 54–55] *Alma, d'après Oskar Kokoschka*, 2007
Exhibition views, *Baltiques*, Kunsthalle Bern, 2012
Photo: Gunnar Meier

[p. 57] Exhibition view, *Carrousel*, La Ferme du Buisson, Noisiel, 2010
With *Les Grimaces d'après Luc Andrié*, 2008, 11 sculptures in plaster, 50 × 35 × 25 cm each, and *Le Must*, 2004, video, sound, 82'51"
Both: Collection Frac Languedoc-Roussillon, Montpellier
Photo: Aurélien Mole

[p. 58] Exhibition view, *Carrousel*, La Ferme du Buisson, Noisiel, 2010
Photo: Aurélien Mole

[p. 59] Exhibition view, *Baltiques*, Kunsthalle Bern, 2012
With *Fontaines*, 2012, and *Le Must*, 2004
Photo: Gunnar Meier

[p. 60] *Marie-Louise*, 2013
Mixed media, 54 × 61 × 43 cm
Production: Evelyne Villaime
Photo: Annik Wetter

[p. 64] *Fernando*, 2012
Mixed media, 35 × 35 × 44 cm
Production: Evelyne Villaime
Photo: Annik Wetter

Biography

Born in 1981 in Granges-Marnand (Switzerland), Denis Savary lives and works in Paris and Geneva. He graduated from ECAL, Lausanne, in 2004. He received the Swiss Federal Art Prize in 2011, and was awarded a residency at Palais de Tokyo, Paris, in 2006–2007. He is represented by Xippas Gallery, Paris/Geneva/Montevideo.

SELECTED SOLO EXHIBITIONS

2013

Les Mannequins de Corot, Musée d'Art et d'Histoire, Geneva
Étourneaux, Le Cyclop, Milly-la-Forêt
Étrusques, Art3, Valence
Xippas Art Contemporain, Geneva

2012

Baltiques, Kunsthalle Bern, Bern

2011

Un balcon en forêt, with Jean-Yves Jouannais, Galerie du Granit/Scène nationale, Belfort
Brûlis, Galerie Xippas, Paris
Period Room, Galerie Evergreene, Geneva
… Philippe Ramette … , with Philippe Ramette, CRAC, Sète

2010

Carrousel, Centre d'art contemporain de La Ferme du Buisson, Noisiel
Les Mannequins de Corot, performance, Swiss Cultural Center, Paris
Les Mannequins de Corot, performance, Musée d'Art et d'Histoire, Geneva
Le Narrenschiff, Centre PasquArt, Biel/Bienne
La Villa, Villa Bernasconi, Grand-Lancy/Geneva*
Victorine, performance with Delphine Lorenzo, Festival EXTRA-BALL, Swiss Cultural Center, Paris

2009

Les Mannequins de Corot, performance, Le Printemps de Septembre, Musée des Augustins, Toulouse

2008

Billard, Galerie Evergreene, Geneva
Galerie Xippas, Athens
Meilleurs vœux, Jeu de Paume, Paris*

2007

Musée Jenisch Vevey, Vevey*
Galerie Xippas, Paris

2005

Elles portent des plaisirs qui leur sont propres mais qui n'ont rien à voir avec le plaisir de se gratter, La Russille
Perpetual Motion Food, Sima Gallery, Nuremberg

SELECTED GROUP EXHIBITIONS

2013

L'Origine des choses, Centre national des arts plastiques Collection, Centrale for Contemporary Art, Brussels*
LOST IN LA, Los Angeles Municipal Art Gallery, Los Angeles*
Hors Pistes, screening, Centre Pompidou, Paris; Museu da Imagen e do Som, Sao Paulo
Le Regard du bègue, Mamco, Geneva
Pratiques domestiques, CNEAI, Chatou, with André S. Labarthe and Alexandre Costenzo

2012

La Jeunesse est un art/Manor Art Award Anniversary Exhibition, Kunsthaus Aarau, Aarau
Misia, reine de Paris, Musée d'Orsay, Paris, and Musée Bonnard, Le Cannet*
This and there, 10 ans du Pavillon du Palais de Tokyo, Fondation d'entreprise Ricard, Paris
Re, performance, stage direction by Denis Savary, Théâtre de Vidy, Lausanne

2010

Modèles modèles 2, Mamco, Geneva
Swiss Drawings (1990–2010), Musée Rath, Geneva, and Kunsthaus Aarau, Aarau*

2009

Insiders, pratiques, usages, savoir-faire, Capc–musée d'Art contemporain, Bordeaux
Invasion of Sound, Zacheta National Gallery of Art, Warsaw
Félicien Marboeuf (1852–1924), Fondation d'Entreprise Ricard, Paris*

2006

Incipit, Fondation d'entreprise Ricard, Paris

2005

Scènes de vie, Swiss Cultural Center, Paris*
Disappearance, Fri-Art, Fribourg

2004

33rd International Film Festival, Rotterdam
10e Biennale de l'image en mouvement, Geneva

* Publication

This book has been published in collaboration with

Centre d'art contemporain de La Ferme du Buisson
Allée de la Ferme – Noisiel
77448 Marne-la-Vallée Cedex 2
France
T: + 33 (0)1 64 62 77 00
E: contact@lafermedubuisson.com
www.lafermedubuisson.com

The Centre d'art contemporain de La Ferme du Buisson organized a solo exhibition of Denis Savary entitled *Carrousel* in 2010–2011.

The Centre d'art contemporain de La Ferme du Buisson is supported by: Drac Ile-de-France/Ministère de la Culture et de la Communication; Communauté d'Agglomération du Val-Maubuée; Conseil général de Seine-et-Marne; Conseil régional d'Île-de-France.

A French version of the texts reproduced in this monograph is available at La Ferme du Buisson and Galerie Xippas.

This publication has received the support of

Galerie Xippas
108, rue Vieille-du-Temple
75003 Paris – France
T: + 33 (0)1 40 27 05 55
E: paris@xippas.com
www.xippas.com

Denis Savary wishes to thank all those who contributed, from near or far, to the successful realization of this publication.

PUBLICATION

EDITOR Clément Dirié, with the assistance of Naima Saidi
EDITING AND PROFREADING Clare Manchester
TEXTS Jean-Yves Jouannais, Philippe-Alain Michaud, Julie Pellegrin
TRANSLATIONS Judith Hayward
DESIGN Nicolas Eigenheer & Vera Kaspar
TYPEFACE Hermes (www.optimo.ch)
COLOR SEPARATION & PRINT
Musumeci S.P.A., Quart (Aosta)

Printed in Europe

PUBLISHED BY
JRP|Ringier
Limmatstrasse 270
8005 Zurich
Tel. + 41 (0) 43 311 27 50
Fax + 41 (0) 43 311 27 51
www.jrp-ringier.com
info@jrp-ringier.com

ISBN 978-3-03764-227-6

JRP | Ringier books are available internationally at selected bookstores and from the following distribution partners:

SWITZERLAND
AVA Verlagsauslieferung AG,
Centralweg 16, CH– 8910 Affoltern a.A.
verlagsservice@ava.ch, www.ava.ch

FRANCE
Les presses du réel,
35 rue Colson, F– 21000 Dijon,
info@lespressesdureel.com, www.lespressesdureel.com

GERMANY AND AUSTRIA
Vice Versa Distribution GmbH,
Immanuelkirchstrasse 12, D – 10405 Berlin
info@vice-versa-distribution.com,
www.vice-versa-distribution.com

UK AND OTHER EUROPEAN COUNTRIES
Cornerhouse Publications,
70 Oxford Street, UK– Manchester M1 5NH
publications@cornerhouse.org,
www.cornerhouse.org/books

USA, CANADA, ASIA, AND AUSTRALIA
ARTBOOK|D.A.P.,
155 Sixth Avenue, 2nd Floor, USA–New York, NY 10013
orders@dapinc.com,
www.artbook.com

For a list of our partner bookshops or for any general questions, please contact JRP|Ringier directly at info@jrp-ringier.com, or visit our homepage www.jrp-ringier.com for further information about our program.

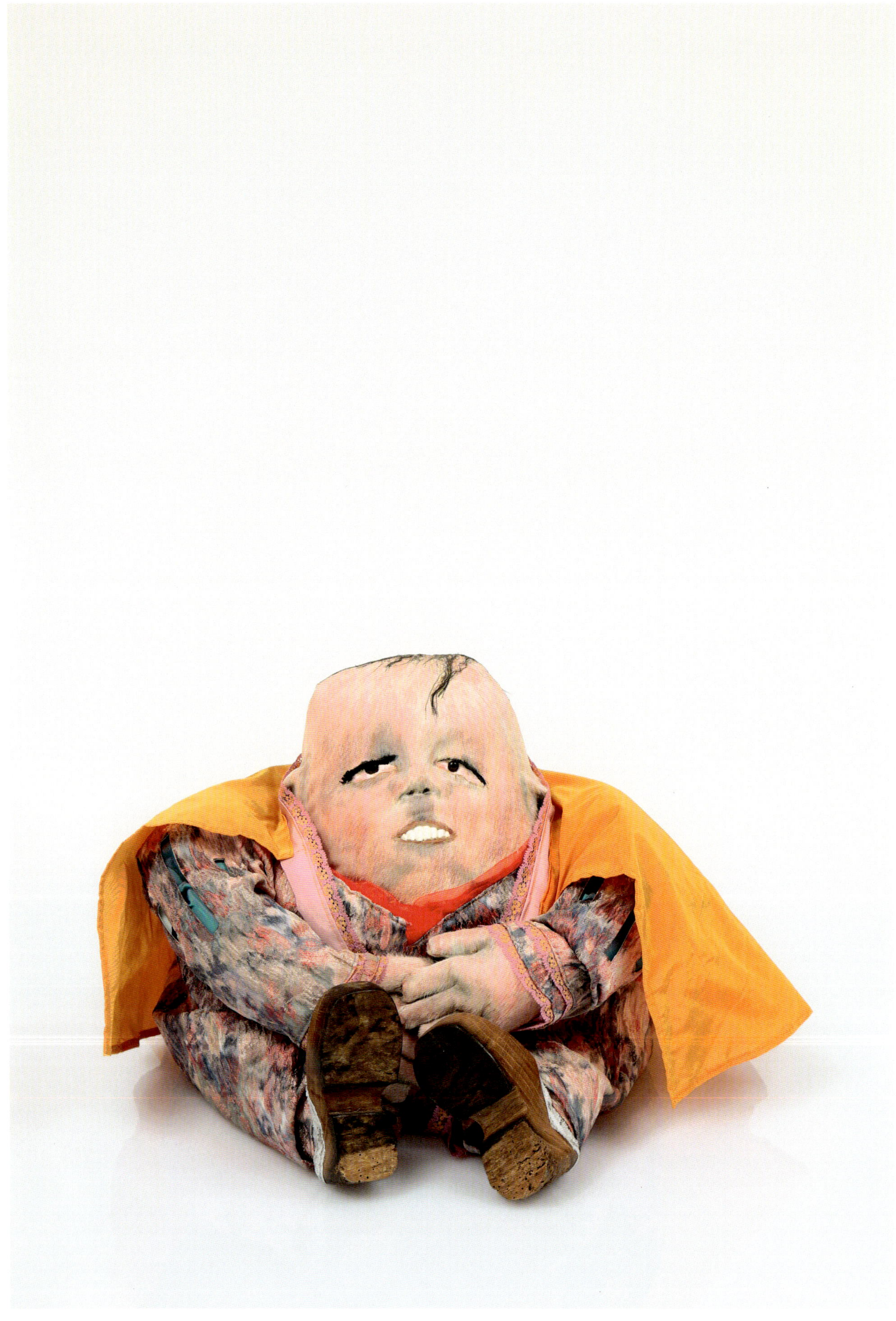

FERNANDO, 2012